mc rainier

A CLIMBING GUIDE

FOREWORD BY BRUCE BARCOTT

Mike Gauthier

THE
MOUNTAINEERS

Published by
The Mountaineers
1001 SW Klickitat Way, Suite 201
Seattle, WA 98134

Published simultaneously in Great Britain by Cordee, 3a DeMontfort Street, Leicester, England, LE1 7HD

Manufactured in Canada

Edited by Don Graydon
Maps and photo correcting by Gray Mouse Graphics
All photographs by the author unless otherwise noted
Cover and book design by Ani Rucki
Book layout by Alice C. Merrill

Cover photographs: *Mountaineering; Joe Puryear climbs through winter conditions high on the Emmons Glacier, August, 1998. Inset: Mount Rainier from the east, Little Tahoma in the foreground.*
Frontispiece: *Crevasses on the Winthrop Glacier, sunrise.*
Dedication page: *David Gottlieb on the Winthrop Glacier landscape.*

Library of Congress Cataloging-in-Publication Data
Gauthier, Mike, 1969–
    Mount Rainier: a climbing guide / by Mike Gauthier. — 1st ed.
        p.   cm.
    "Published simultaneously in Great Britain by Cordee."
    Includes bibliographical references (p.   ) and index.
        1. Mountaineering—Washington (State)—Rainier, Mount Guidebooks.
    2. Rainier, Mount (Wash.) Guidebooks. I. Title.
    GV199.42.W22R344 1999
    796.52'2'09797782—dc21   99–6580
                                                              CIP

DEDICATION

In memory of Jim Brown, Phil Otis, and Sean Ryan

CONTENTS

Foreword ... 7
Acknowledgments ... 9
About the Contributors ... 10

PART I
the mountain

A History of Ascents ... 13
The National Park ... 15
Planning a Successful Climb ... 25
Safety and Survival ... 37
Weather *by Mark Moore* ... 45
Avalanches *by Mark Moore* ... 51
Health *by Jim Litch, M.D.* ... 56
On the Mountain ... 62
How to Use this Guidebook ... 72

PART II
the routes

List of Routes ... 78

Paradise Approaches ... 79
  CAMP MUIR ROUTES ... 79
    Ingraham Glacier Direct and Disappointment Cleaver ... 81
    Gibraltar Ledges (Gib Ledges) ... 84
    Gibraltar Chute (Gib Chute) ... 87
    Nisqually Ice Cliff and Nisqually Cleaver ... 89
    Nisqually Icefall ... 92
  WAPOWETY CLEAVER AND KAUTZ ROUTES ... 93
    Fuhrer Finger and Fuhrer Thumb ... 96
    Wilson Glacier Headwall ... 99
    Kautz Glacier ... 102
    Kautz Headwall ... 105
    Kautz Cleaver ... 107

Longmire and Westside Road Approaches ... 110
  SUCCESS CLEAVER ROUTES ... 112
    Success Couloirs ... 113
    Success Cleaver ... 115
    South Tahoma Headwall ... 117
  TAHOMA CLEAVER ROUTE ... 119
    Tahoma Cleaver ... 120
  PUYALLUP CLEAVER ROUTES ... 124
    Tahoma Glacier and the Sickle ... 126
    Sunset Amphitheater:
        The Ice Cap and Headwall Couloir ... 128
    Sunset Ridge ... 131

Mowich Lake and Carbon River Approaches ... 135
  MOWICH FACE ROUTES ... 137
    Edmunds Headwall ... 139
    Central Mowich Face ... 141
    North Mowich Headwall ... 143
    North Mowich Icefall ... 145
  PTARMIGAN RIDGE ROUTES ... 146
    Ptarmigan Ridge and Ice Cliff ... 148

White River Approaches ... 152
  LOWER CURTIS RIDGE ROUTES ... 152
    Liberty Wall: The Ice Cap and Direct ... 156
    Liberty Ridge ... 158
    Willis Wall: Thermogenesis ... 161
    Willis Wall: West Rib ... 163
    Willis Wall: Central Rib ... 164
    Willis Wall: East Rib ... 167
    Willis Wall: East Willis Wall ... 170
    Curtis Ridge ... 171
  CAMP SCHURMAN ROUTES ... 173
    Winthrop Glacier/Russell Cliffs ... 174
    Emmons/Winthrop Glaciers ... 176

Appendix I: Glossary of Selected Mountaineering Terms ... 181
Appendix II: Suggested Reading and Other Information Sources ... 183
Index ... 185

FOREWORD

We were just below Pebble Creek, about to slog up the vanilla plain of the Muir snowfield, when Mike greeted a bandana'd hiker and his friend grubbing some cashews.

"How you guys doing today?" he asked.

"We're doing great, man," said Banadana Boy, wiping the late July sweat from his cheek. "How could we not? We're on Rainier!"

He said it as if we had all rounded a corner and stumbled upon the spot where God had stashed Eden all these years. And in a way, we had. At our feet the heathers, all pinks and whites, were beginning to reclaim the Paradise Valley from the winter's eight-month freeze. To our left the Nisqually Glacier's crevasses split open like creamy wounds in snow unsoiled by the summer's rockfall. Behind us not a single cloud obscured the view of the Tatoosh and southern Cascades. And before us stood Rainier, big and fat and available, blocking out half the postcard sky. This is what makes this place so damn wonderful and so damn dangerous, makes people around here behold this mountain like a god and love it like a grandmother. Mike put it in technical terms: Ripper day.

It's a day like this that makes people take Rainier too lightly, makes them plan a two-day summit run, makes them turn tail and run in shock when a front moves in from the Pacific and spanks every living thing above 6,000 feet. Because the truth of the matter is, this is one hell of a deceptive mountain. On the right day a fit climber may zigzag up the cleaver with no hassle from the gods of wind, rain, and snow. Thing is, we don't get too many right days around here. Most are wrong ten ways from Tuesday. The altitude you may plan for, the endurance you can train for, the will you must summon, but the weather can only be gambled with. There are plenty of other fourteen-thousanders on the continent, but none that will give you the wild ride of Rainier.

One bit of advice: Take your rewards along the way. Take them on the White River trail in to Glacier Basin, at midnight under the stars at Camp Muir, at dawn on Disappointment Cleaver, at midmorning astride an Emmons Glacier crevasse. Emulate John Muir, who lounged in Rainier's mountain meadows on his way to the top, gazing at the mountain "in silent admiration, buried in tall daisies and anemones by the side of a snowbank." The summit may hold some personal triumph, but it does not promise splendors for the eye. You may see nothing but the hazy outline of your climbing partners, or you may catch a glimpse of the tableau that struck Hazard Stevens, the first recorded climber to reach the summit, with awe. "The wind," he wrote, "was now a perfect tempest, and bitterly cold; smoke and mist were flying about the base of the mountain, half hiding, half revealing its gigantic outlines; and the whole scene was sublimely awful."

The American alpinist Alex Lowe once said there were two kinds of climbers: "Those who climb because their heart sings when they're in the mountains, and all the rest." Your guide up Rainier's many faces is one whose heart sings arias. Mike Gauthier is an old-school climber in a young man's body, a mountaineer who's spent one third of his life on Rainier. He has been to the top of this mountain more than 150 times, and in one punishing summer season recorded thirty six summits—if you do the math, that works out to a run to Columbia Crest every sixty hours or so. Like the bandana'd fellow that day on the trail, when he's on Rainier, Mike's doing great, man. He picks up his mail in the mountain lowlands but his true home is 10,000 feet high, at Camp Muir and Camp Schurman, where he plies his trade as a national park climbing ranger. If the mountain's glaciers contain the story of every climber who's crossed them, Mike Gauthier has left volumes of joy and sorrow on the faces of Rainier. From him I've learned to distrust the mountain while loving every minute I spend upon it, to use wisdom and prudence and boldness when traveling its flanks, and to have the best time possible under the worst conditions imaginable. Some days I see the summit from Seattle and wonder if he's up there hunkered down against the tempest in the sublimely awful scene. Most days he is.

Bruce Barcott
Seattle, Washington
August, 1999

ACKNOWLEDGMENTS

This guide would be incomplete without the input and assistance of many kind people, all of whom care very much about Mount Rainier. I would like to recognize the contributions from those who live, work, and study on the mountain for the National Park Service. Your Mount Rainier experience and advice were irreplaceable to this guide: Mike Carney, Rick Kirschner, Uwe Nehring, Garry Olson, Regina Rochefort, Barbara Samora, Darin Swinney, John Wilcox, Steve Winslow, and the Mount Rainier Climbing Rangers. A special thanks to Sheri Forbes for her backstop review.

To those who aided me in a variety of ways: answering questions, offering suggestions, flying me around, reviewing text, and going the extra mile, thank you very much: Rachel Bishop, Skip Card, Jess Jagerman, Scott Hacker, John Kissell, Bob Krimmel, Jack Leicester, Donald Ross, Josh Silverstein, Roger Ternes, and Doug Uttecht. Similarly, I praise the entire staff of The Mountaineers Books for their skilled assistance in producing this guide. It was a pleasure to work with Cindy Bohn, Helen Cherullo, Kathleen Cubley, Margaret Foster, Don Graydon, Alison Koop, Ani Rucki, and Margaret Sullivan.

Many climbers have shared their thoughts, feelings, and stories about Mount Rainier with me. Their personal insights were a highlight during this project and I look forward to seeing them again on the mountain: Alex Bertulis, Eddie Boulton, Dan Davis, Dawes Eddy, Jon Olson, Allen Sanderson, Eric Simonson, Peter Whittaker, and Jim Wickwire.

Very big thanks are in order to Jim Litch and Mark Moore. Their specialized expertise added professional voice and gives climbers insightful information about safely ascending Mount Rainier. And to Bruce Barcott, your encouragement and assistance were very much appreciated.

Finally, my deepest gratitude goes to the friends and climbing partners who have shared time on Mount Rainier with me. Our adventures were invaluable and your personalities have indelibly marked my work. Thank you for your patience, understanding, support, and inspiration: George Beilstein, Lara Bitenieks, David Gottlieb, Chad Kellog, Stefan Lofgren, Tom Mallard, Dee Patterson, Joe Puryear, and Mark Westman.

Mike Gauthier

ABOUT THE CONTRIBUTORS

Dr. Jim Litch has climbed and guided several 8,000-meter peaks, including Mount Everest. He is a veteran of twenty-two other expeditions worldwide and seventy-eight ascents of Mount Rainier. A former climbing ranger for Mount Rainier and Denali National Parks, Jim has worked rescues on five continents including Antarctica. He has published more than two dozen articles on high altitude medicine and conducts research and lectures throughout North America, Europe, and Asia. Jim currently lives at 13,000 feet in the Mount Everest region of Nepal running a hospital and health care system for Sherpas.

Mark Moore became interested in snow and mountain weather as a professional ski patroller in the early 1970s. After obtaining a master's degree in atmospheric sciences, Mark helped found the Northwest Weather and Avalanche Center in Seattle, Washington, and has been its director since 1988. He has instructed at the U.S. National Avalanche School, Northwest Avalanche Institute, American Avalanche Institute, and Alaska Avalanche School, and has authored numerous articles on mountain weather and avalanches. An avid skier, snowboarder, and outdoor enthusiast, he likes to experience what he forecasts—right or wrong.

Facing page: A windblown Arctic landscape, Mount Rainier, winter

the mountain

Mount Rainier in the early morning autumn light

Experienced mountaineers and novice climbers alike test their mettle on Mount Rainier. Steep glacial ice and huge crevasses challenge routefinding and technical skills. The thin air of high altitude strains every climber's constitution. Storms from the Pacific bring heavy snowfall, whiteouts, and fierce winds.

Such demanding conditions are among those that climbers may experience, but it's the chance for success and the pleasures of mountaineering that are the lures. Limitless views, spectacular sunrises, expansive glaciers, mysterious crevasses, and the possibility of standing on the summit are some of the joys that attract climbers.

The spectacular beauty coupled with rigorous mountaineering conditions also makes Rainier an excellent training ground. Whether you're preparing to climb an even more challenging peak or just want to practice mountaineering skills, Rainier has it all. Within a day's hike from your car, you can experience technical climbing on snow and ice, high altitude, and glaciers—the largest glacial system on any peak in the lower forty-eight states. A panorama that includes Mount Hood in Oregon plus Mount St. Helens and Mount Adams in Washington is an hour's walk from the Paradise Ranger Station.

At a height of 14,410 feet (4,392 meters), this massive volcano dwarfs nearby mountains and can be viewed from Canada to central Oregon. Swollen rivers fed by glaciers divide its flanks. Its lower hills are forested with old-growth Douglas-firs, cedars, and hemlocks. Summer meadows attract botanists, photographers, and those seeking an escape from urban life. "The mountain," as local residents refer to Rainier, is a Pacific Northwest icon, and a weather forecast can be obtained by simply asking if "the mountain" is out. With its raw beauty, easy access, and high challenge, it's no wonder that thousands of climbers each year attempt to reach the summit.

A HISTORY OF ASCENTS

Climbers have been attracted to Mount Rainier since at least the mid-nineteenth century, with recorded climbing attempts beginning in 1852. Two surveyors, whose names are not known, ascended via the Emmons and Winthrop Glaciers, probably in 1855. Their accurate description of the summit crater and its steam caves makes their ascent believable, though little else is known of the climb. In July 1857, a party led by Lieutenant August Valentine Kautz reached the high slopes of the upper mountain.

General Hazard Stevens and Philemon Beecher Van Trump are credited with the first documented ascent. Climbing for 11 hours from their timberline camp on August 17, 1870, the pair reached the summit. Arriving late in the day, they were forced to spend the night inside one of the summit crater ice caves, next to the warmth of a steam vent.

Mountaineer's sunrise on Emmons Glacier

Other notable ascents include John Muir's climb in 1888, when A. C. Warner took the first photographs of the summit and its crater. In 1890, Fay Fuller became the first woman to climb Mount Rainier. By the turn of the century, about 160 mountaineers had reached the top.

Summit attempts became more and more popular, with the number totaling more than a thousand in 1961—about 600 of them successful ascents. During the late 1950s, '60s, and '70s, climbing fever took hold. Many of Rainier's more difficult routes, like the Willis Wall, Curtis Ridge, and Tahoma Cleaver, saw first ascents. Competition among climbers to complete new ascent lines and variations was fierce. By 1979, nearly 8,000 climbers were attempting the peak each year. By then virtually every climbing line had been ascended, many during the winter.

Mount Rainier attracts climbers now more than ever, with top athletes pushing new limits. Unfinished winter routes, speed climbs, and ski and snowboard descents challenge today's adventurer. On September 1, 1998, climbing ranger Chad Kellogg went from the Paradise trailhead at an elevation of 5,420 feet to the 14,410-foot summit and back in 5 hours and 6 minutes—a trip that takes the average climber a good 2 days. Backcountry snowboarders carve turns on steep headwalls and glaciers, while ski mountaineers circumnavigate the mammoth peak in less than 3 days. There is always something new to strive toward on Mount Rainier.

More than 11,000 climbers a year now attempt the mountain, with a success rate of about 50 percent. Summit climbs that took weeks in the late nineteenth century are now routinely completed in 2 or 3 days. Times have changed and so has the way we play on Mount Rainier. High-tech gear, paved roads, advanced climbing techniques, instant weather and route information, and extensive knowledge of the terrain and geology make the dream of climbing Mount Rainier a possibility for many.

THE NATIONAL PARK

Mount Rainier is managed and protected by the National Park Service. The 235,625 acres of Mount Rainier National Park provide recreational opportunities for the million-plus people of the neighboring Puget Sound metropolitan area and for visitors from around the world.

RANGER STATIONS AND INFORMATION CENTERS

Several ranger stations and other facilities provide services and information useful to climbers.

Paradise Climbing Ranger Station. At the upper end of the upper parking lot at Paradise; 360-569-2211, Ext. 2314; open daily in summer. Climbing rangers staff the station in the mornings, providing permits and route and weather information. This is the best place to call for current reports on climbing

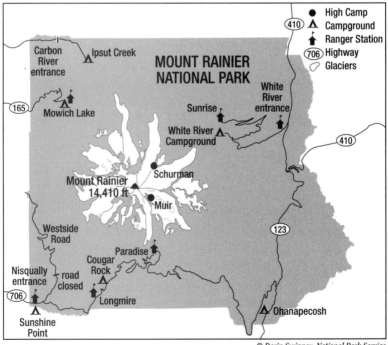

© *Darin Swinney, National Park Service*

conditions. During periods when the station is not staffed, phone callers can listen to recorded information.

Henry M. Jackson Visitor Center. The large, round building at Paradise; 360-569-2211, Ext. 2328; open daily from early May to mid-October; weekends and holidays the rest of the year. This is the main visitor and information center for the park. National Park interpretive rangers provide a wide variety of information for all visitors, and the center houses interpretive displays about the park's cultural and natural history. You can get a climbing permit here when the Paradise Climbing Ranger Station is closed. The Jackson Visitor Center has the only public shower facilities in the entire park. The showers are on the lower level. Bring quarters; it's worth it.

Longmire Museum and Longmire Wilderness Information Center. These two facilities are near each other at the upper end of Longmire; 360-569-4453 or 360-569-2211, Ext. 3317, April through September, and Ext. 3314, October through March; open daily year-round. Rangers provide permits and information to climbers and other backcountry users on the south and west sides of the park. Go to the museum during periods when the main center is closed.

White River Ranger Station. One mile west of State Route 410, on the White River–Sunrise road on the east side of the park; 360-569-2211, Ext. 2356; open daily from late May to mid-October. Rangers provide permits and climbing and backcountry information for the north and east sides of the park.

Wilkeson Ranger Station. In the town of Wilkeson, on State Route 165, 13 miles before the Carbon River entrance at the northwest corner of the park; 360-569-2211, Ext. 2358; open daily in summer. Rangers provide permits and climbing and backcountry information for the north and west sides of the park.

Mailing address for park headquarters is Mount Rainier National Park, Tahoma Woods, Star Route, Ashford, WA 98304-9751. A call to the main number, 360-569-2211, provides an automated voice menu that gives access to basic recorded information or to the extension numbers of other park offices. The main switchboard extension is 2334.

Internet site for information on climbing at Mount Rainier is www.nps.gov/mora/climb.htm. The e-mail address for Mount Rainier National Park is morainfo@nps.gov.

GETTING TO THE PARK

Mount Rainier National Park has excellent road access from all directions in summer. Many roads are closed in winter. An entrance fee of $10 pays for a single-vehicle pass valid for 7 days. A Mount Rainier pass good for one year

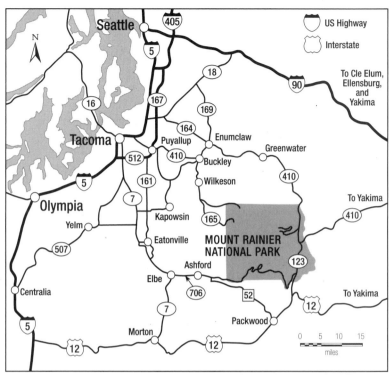

Puget Sound Regional Map © Darin Swinney, National Park Service

from month of purchase is available for $20. A $50 Golden Eagle pass is valid at all national parks for one year from month of purchase. Prices are as of 1999.

Following are directions to the park from the metropolitan areas of Seattle, Portland, and Yakima.

PARADISE, LONGMIRE, AND WESTSIDE ROAD CLIMBING ACCESS

Routes on the south and west sides of the mountain are accessed from Seattle or Portland through the Nisqually entrance in the southwest corner of the park—the only entrance open year-round. Access to the routes from Yakima in eastern Washington is through the Stevens Canyon entrance in the park's southeast corner, closed in winter.

From Seattle: Take I-5 south to I-405. Go east 3 miles on I-405 and then take State Route 167 south 21 miles to State Route 512. Drive on State Route 512 for 3 miles, exiting right onto State Route 161 south. Drive south on State Route 161 through Puyallup and Graham to Eatonville. Turn left at the stop sign in Eatonville (look for the Mount Rainier signs) and follow the two-lane country road to its end at a T. From the T, turn left on State Route 7 and continue to Elbe. Stay left on State Route 706 in Elbe and drive 13 miles east through Ashford to the Nisqually entrance of Mount Rainier National Park. The park road from here to Longmire and Paradise is kept open year-round.

From Portland: Take I-5 north to U.S. Hwy. 12. Head east for 30 miles to Morton, then north 17 miles on State Route 7 to Elbe. Connect with State Route 706 in Elbe and travel east for 13 miles to the Nisqually entrance.

From Yakima: Take State Route 410 from Yakima for 18 miles, and turn left on U.S. Hwy. 12. Follow U.S. 12 for 47 miles to State Route 123. Turn right on State Route 123, heading north for 6 miles to the Stevens Canyon entrance. Turn left here onto State Route 706 (Stevens Canyon Road) and follow the signs to Paradise or Longmire. (Routes 410 and 123 and Stevens Canyon Road are closed in winter due to heavy snowfall.)

MOWICH LAKE AND CARBON RIVER CLIMBING ACCESS

Routes on the northwest side of Mount Rainier should be accessed from Mowich Lake.

From Seattle: Take I-5 south to I-405. Go east 3 miles on I-405 and then take State Route 167 south, following it 11 miles to State Route 18 and the Auburn exit. Follow Route 18 for 1 mile to State Route 164, getting off at the Auburn-Enumclaw exit. Take a left at the stoplight onto State Route 164 heading east to Enumclaw, where the highway will T against State Route 410. Turn right (west) at the stoplight and go 4 miles to Buckley, where you'll go left on State Route 165. Follow Route 165 through Wilkeson and Carbonado and beyond to a one-lane bridge crossing followed by a fork in the road. Stay to the right, continuing 17 miles on the unpaved road to Mowich Lake. (If going to Ipsut Creek Campground, stay left at the fork and continue 16 miles up the Carbon River road.)

From Portland: Take I-5 north to exit 127, State Route 512. Stay in the right-hand lane on Route 512 as it becomes State Route 167 north. Continue in the right lane for 1 mile and then exit onto State Route 410. Follow Route 410 east for 11 miles to Buckley, there turning right onto State Route 165. Follow Route 165 through Wilkeson and Carbonado and beyond to a one-lane bridge crossing followed by a fork in the road. Stay to the right, continuing 17 miles on the unpaved road to Mowich Lake. (If going to Ipsut Creek Campground, stay left at the fork and continue 16 miles up the Carbon River road.)

From Yakima: Take State Route 410 from Yakima for 69 miles to the east park entrance, at Chinook Pass. Continue on Route 410 for 46 miles around the north end of the park to Buckley, where you'll turn left on State Route

165. Follow Route 165 through Wilkeson and Carbonado and beyond to a one-lane bridge crossing followed by a fork in the road. Stay to the right, continuing 17 miles on the unpaved road to Mowich Lake. (If going to Ipsut Creek Campground, stay left at the fork and continue 16 miles up the Carbon River road.)

WHITE RIVER CLIMBING ACCESS

The White River area provides the best entry and exit (descent) for routes on the north and northeast sides of the mountain.

From Seattle and Portland: Get onto State Route 410 (see driving directions above for Mowich Lake). Stay on Route 410 to the park boundary and arch, 31 miles east of Enumclaw. Continue 5 miles to the White River–Sunrise turnoff, where you'll go right. The White River Ranger Station and entrance booth is 1 mile down the road.

From Yakima: Take State Route 410 from Yakima for 69 miles to the east park entrance, at Chinook Pass. Continue 7 miles along State Route 410 and turn left (west) at the White River–Sunrise turnoff. The White River Ranger Station and entrance booth is 1 mile down the road.

Most of the park's climbing access roads are closed in winter. These include State Routes 410 and 123 within the park, Stevens Canyon Road (State Route 706 between Narada Falls and State Route 123), and the Mowich Lake road. The only road access to the park during late fall, winter, and spring is through the Nisqually entrance. If you intend to climb a route on the east, north, or west side at these times, you'll have to ski or snowshoe along the closed road.

Three vendors provide transportation services from the Seattle area. Grayline bus service offers regular tour schedules to the park from downtown Seattle. For information, call 1-800-426-7532 or 206-626-5208. Rainier Overland operates a shuttle between Seattle-Tacoma International Airport and the town of Ashford and locations within the park. Call 360-569-2604. Rainier Shuttle operates scheduled runs between the airport and Paradise with a stop in Ashford. Call 360-569-2331.

CAMPING AND LODGING

Four of the park's campgrounds charge a fee of $10 to $14 per night; there is no charge for use of the Ipsut Creek or Mowich Lake Campgrounds. The Cougar Rock and Ohanapecosh Campgrounds require a reservation from July 1 through Labor Day weekend. Call 1-800-365-CAMP, 301-722-1257, or 1-888-530-9796 TDD, or write to National Park Reservation Service, P.O. Box 1600,

Cumberland, MD 21502. Other campgrounds are first-come, first-served. No campground has showers or RV hookups. There are public showers on the lower floor of the Henry M. Jackson Visitor Center at Paradise.

Sunshine Point Campground is half a mile inside the Nisqually entrance, at an elevation of 2,000 feet. It has 18 individual sites; open year-round.

Cougar Rock Campground is 2.3 miles north of Longmire, at an elevation of 3,180 feet. It has 200 individual sites and 5 group sites; open late May to mid-October. Sites may be available upon arrival without reservations if the campground is not full (often the case Sunday through Wednesday nights).

Ohanapecosh Campground is 3 miles north of the southeast park boundary, at an elevation of 1,914 feet. It has 205 individual sites; open late May to mid-October. Sites may be available upon arrival without reservations if the campground is not full (often the case Sunday through Wednesday nights).

White River Campground is 5 miles west of the White River entrance off State Route 410, at an elevation of 4,400 feet. It has 112 individual sites; open mid-June to late September.

Ipsut Creek Campground is 6 miles east of the Carbon River entrance in the northwest corner of the park, at an elevation of 2,300 feet. It has 28 individual campsites; open year-round, depending on snow conditions.

Mowich Lake Campground is in the northwest corner of the park at the end of State Route 165, at an elevation of 4,929 feet. It has 30 walk-in-only sites, about 50 yards from where you park the car; open mid-May to mid-October.

The two hotels in the park are managed by Mount Rainier Guest Services. The National Park Inn at Longmire is open year-round. The Paradise Inn at Paradise is open mid-May to early October. Both hotels have a full-service restaurant, lounge, and gift shop. For reservations, call 360-569-2275 or write to Mount Rainier Guest Services, P.O. Box 108, Ashford, WA 98304. Their Internet address is www.guestservices.com/rainier.

CLIMBING PERMITS

Climbing teams must register and get a permit from the National Park Service before leaving the trailhead. A special-use fee of $15 per person (or $25 per person for an annual pass) is collected from those intending to climb or travel above high camp. Teams can register in person at any of the ranger stations or wilderness information centers listed above. For an additional fee of $20 per party, reservations can be made as much as 60 days in advance of the climb by calling 360-569-4453 (or by fax at 360-569-2255 or e-mail at mora_wilderness@nps.gov).

Rangers at Camp Schurman, discussing route conditions with climbers

Climbing fees help pay for projects that assist climbing on the mountain, including solar-assisted outhouses at Camp Schurman and Camp Muir and helicopter flights to remove the waste. Fees are also directed to the climbing Web page and other public information services and to salaries for climbing rangers.

In registering, a team fills out a card with information on the dates of the trip, intended route, high camp, emergency contacts, essential gear, team members, and climbing experience. If space is available at the intended high camp, the ranger will register the team and file the information card until the climbers return and check out. Data on the card is used if the team becomes seriously overdue or needs rescue.

If your team tries to register for a high camp that is already at permitted capacity, you'll be asked to choose another route or to come back later. You can avoid this problem by climbing during midweek or off-season or by selecting a lightly traveled route. If you must climb on a busy summer weekend or holiday, arrive early and have a backup route. The Park Service requires solo climbers to obtain written permission from a permanent climbing ranger before ascending the peak. Additionally, climbers under the age of eighteen must provide written permission from a parent or guardian. Both policies are under review and may be changed, call first to check.

Parties may camp for a maximum of 14 days in the backcountry. Maximum party size is twelve people, with any team larger than five considered a group party. There are limits on the number of people allowed in many of the high camps and alpine zones. Following are limits for the most popular high camps:

Muir Snowfield	36 people
Camp Muir	110 people
Ingraham Flats	35 people
Camp Hazard	36 people
Kautz Alpine Zone	36 people
Inter Glacier (snow only)	2 parties
Glacier Basin	5 regular parties; 1 group party
Camp Schurman	48 people
Emmons Flats	24 people
Thumb Rock	12 people
Rainier Summit	36 people

Providing a guided climb or mountaineering instruction in exchange for money is illegal within the park, except by one of the following authorized concession services.

Alpine Ascents International: 206-378-1927
American Alpine Institute: 360-671-1505
Cascade Alpine Guides: 206-706-1587
Mount Rainier Alpine Guides: 360-825-3773
Rainier Mountaineering Inc.: 253-627-6242

PROTECTING THE PARK

The National Park Service manages wilderness areas "in such manner as will leave them unimpaired for future use and enjoyment. . . . " Some 97 percent of Mount Rainier National Park is designated by law as wilderness through the Washington Wilderness Act of 1988.

The park owes its existence in part to the efforts of early explorers and mountaineers. They viewed the mountain as a place worth preserving and lobbied to

Climbing to Gibraltar Ledges, in spring conditions, with Mount Adams in the background.

save it from abusive development. But as the park celebrated its centennial birthday in 1999, the pressures of human activity were greater than ever.

Climbers have increasing reason to consider how their actions might affect the wilderness. Standard routes are clogged on summer weekends, and once-pristine areas are starting to shows the signs of climbing use and distress. Issues such as human waste, overcrowding, and wilderness protection are paramount today.

The challenge to today's climber is to embrace the principle of leave-no-trace mountaineering. The leave-no-trace ethic means taking nothing from the mountain and leaving nothing behind—no gear, garbage, climbing wands, food, or anything else. It means the climber avoids creating new tent platforms or rock walls, builds no campfires, and keeps off the fragile alpine plants and meadows. The climber packs along a bag for garbage and carries "blue bags" for human waste (see the later section on blue bags and sanitation). The goal is to leave no sign of your presence, no clue that you were ever there. This isn't so difficult if you think about what you're doing and ask yourself what impacts you might be having.

The wilderness is vital to our culture, an essential component of our history and identity. Mount Rainier provides a major climb that many mountaineers want to check off their list. It also stands as a vital part of America's priceless legacy of wilderness.

PLANNING A SUCCESSFUL CLIMB

Good planning and preparation enhance the success and enjoyment of a Mount Rainier climb. Begin with an honest analysis of your mountaineering skills. Rainier is a technical climb requiring a high degree of self-reliance. If you're new to climbing, consider instruction through a mountaineering school or guide service. Or if you're lucky, you have friends with a lot of mountain climbing experience who can help you learn the fundamentals of crevasse rescue, routefinding, alpine campcraft, and other mountaineering skills.

Mountaineering is a mental exercise as much as a physical event. Mountaineers use their mental and physical faculties, aided by equipment, to achieve climbing objectives. Sound judgment and efficiency are among the best skills to possess as you plan a Rainier climb. The ability to recognize and evaluate

Climbing teams making their way up the lower Emmons Glacier

dangerous situations is a critical mountaineering skill. Mountaineers constantly assess the abilities of all team members and the changing conditions on the mountain to ensure safety and success.

Skilled mountaineers know their own strengths and weaknesses. Climbing with confidence (but not foolish pride) helps to avoid hardships and enables many experienced teams to succeed under adverse conditions. It's dangerous to pin your climbing hopes on fate, allowing luck or other climbing teams to help you make it through. Success is built on independence and realistic self-confidence.

Choosing teammates is an important preparatory step. You will be spending at least 2 days with your teammates on the mountain, in the close confines of a tent or on the rope as you cross dangerous terrain. To ensure you trust your partners' skills and judgment, climb other peaks with them before attempting Rainier. Other glaciated mountains such as Mount Hood, Mount Adams, and Mount Baker are excellent choices. Become familiar with your partners' habits, skills, strengths, and weaknesses. Remember that these people are your best resources if you need help in an emergency. They will share every step of the climb and greatly affect your success and enjoyment.

Do everything you can to be physically prepared for the challenge of Rainier. The climb is incredibly demanding, and lack of physical conditioning may be the largest factor in not reaching the summit.

Aerobic conditioning is vitally important. Hiking up hills with a 50-pound pack is good training. Bicycle riding can also help, and many avid bicyclists do quite well on the mountain. Whatever your form of aerobic exercise, do it four times a week for an hour or more each time. Get your heart pumping, and push hard. The dividends will pay off on your summit attempt. The slopes of the mountain are a bad place to discover that you're not in adequate physical condition or that the mountaineering skills of yourself or your teammates are not up to the demands of Rainier.

Whether climbing Rainier is a once-in-a-lifetime experience for you or just one more affair as part of a life-long passion for mountaineering, the demands are the same. The indifference of the mountain levels the playing field, and the same hazards confront inexperienced and veteran climbers alike. Beginners in all sports make mistakes, but the mistakes typically don't cost them their lives. The sport of climbing, however, is always played at full strength, with no handicaps or special consideration for beginners, no allowance for poor skills.

For dedicated climbers, mountaineering means more than merely ascending a peak. Mountaineering is a pursuit, a way of life, and a state of being. It's living, traveling, exploring, and coexisting within the mountains—off the trails and in the high places of the world. It's about goals, personal accomplishments, friendships, failures, and successes. Sometimes it's about survival. And when the climb is completed, summit or not, you look to the next adventure.

Public interest in mountain climbing has always been high. Adventure and life-threatening danger create mountaineering's romantic image. Yet anyone who has climbed Rainier knows there is no glamour in wearing the same clothing for days, eating marginal food out of a pot, or sleeping next to a snoring, smelly partner. Mount Rainier is a place where climbers put up with a rudimentary physical existence while pushing toward the extraordinary opportunity to stand on the summit.

In preparing for Rainier, some climbers set out to "conquer" the mountain. But there's no reason to confuse Rainier as a challenge with Rainier as an adversary. The mountain can't be "conquered," but it *can* provide a place for testing one's mettle and for pushing personal limits. The true reward is

Climbing the broken Winthrop Glacier in autumn.

just being there, ready to confidently proceed toward achieving the goal. Enjoy the experiences along the way. If you don't reach the summit, you'll still have the experience. And if the summit is an important goal, the mountain will always be there for future attempts.

As you plan your Rainier venture, you can look forward to much more than simply physical hardship and climbing challenge. Also expect your share of relaxation and mental recuperation amid the clean air, silence, and beautiful vistas. Even tent-bound days can be a welcome reprieve from traffic jams, appointments, and the stresses of school or job. Working with teammates toward a common goal forms strong bonds. Triumphs and losses, conversations and stories—all create the fabric of invaluable memories. Mountaineering is extremely demanding, but the joys and rewards outweigh all hardship.

EQUIPMENT AND CLOTHING

Mountaineering, like scuba diving, relies upon specialized gear and clothing for surviving extreme environmental conditions. The gear you bring will depend largely on the season, your experience, and on the route you intend to climb. You may be tempted to bring every piece of gear that might come in handy, but remember that weight is your enemy. A heavy pack can compromise both comfort and safety. On the other hand, be sure you have the proper gear to ascend the peak safely at your skill level. You don't want to be caught out at night with a dead headlamp battery, or on the glacier at noon without sunglasses. The Mountaineers recommend carrying the following ten essentials on every hike: extra clothing, extra food, a pair of sunglasses, a knife, fire starters, a first-aid kit, matches in a waterproof container, a flashlight, a map, and a compass.

You can buy or rent many last-minute items for a Rainier climb at Summit Haus, an outdoors store in Ashford (360-569-2142). The Rainier Mountaineering guide service at Paradise sells basic items such as maps, sunglasses, and water bottles, and rents plastic mountaineering boots, crampons, and ice axes; supplies are limited, however, so call ahead (360-569-2227). It's best to buy all food for the climb before heading to the park, which offers only limited grocery items at the Longmire General Store.

The following lists give a rundown on gear and clothing you should consider for a Rainier climb. I have never carried everything on this list at once, but I have carried each of these items at one time or another for a specific reason. Choose the items you will carry, based on the season, the route, and your style of climbing. Don't be overly concerned if you don't have the best pack, boots, Gore-Tex jacket, or ice tool. Just make sure that what you have works when you need it.

PERSONAL GEAR

Backpack (4,000 to 5,000 cubic-inch capacity)

Sleeping bag (for summer, a synthetic-filled bag rated between 20 and 40 degrees Fahrenheit; for winter, a synthetic or down bag rated between zero and 20 degrees Fahrenheit)

Insulating pad

Water bottles

Headlamp (with extra batteries and bulb)

Flashlight

Crampons

Helmet

Ice ax

Harness

Belay/rappel device

Rescue pulley

Snowshoes or skis

Ski poles

Runners (loops of webbing or cordage)

Rope-ascending system (mechanical ascenders work best for climbing out of a crevasse)

Carabiners

Knife

Compass

Map

Sunglasses or goggles

Sunscreen and lip protection

First-aid kit

Cup, bowl, spoon

Matches and fire starter

Plastic bags

Mountaineering boots (plastic or leather)

Socks (two pairs)

Long underwear, top and bottom (lightweight to midweight for summer, midweight to expedition-weight for winter)

Shorts

Insulating shirt

Synthetic pile jacket

Wind, snow, or rain jacket

Insulating pants

Wind, snow, or rain bibs or pants
Insulating hat
Sun-protection hat
Gloves or mittens (two pairs)
Gaiters
Specialized medication (prescription, allergy, etc.)
Toilet paper
Chemical heat packs for warming extremities
Book
Playing cards
Earplugs
Camera and film
Journal and pen

GROUP GEAR

Tent or bivy sacks
Stove, cookset, and fuel (one pint per two people per day)
Ropes (60-meter rope for a team of four or five people; 50-meter rope for a
team of two to four people)
Snow and ice protection (one snow picket per person, one to five ice screws
per party, one or two snow flukes per party)
Climbing wands (25-100 for summer, 100-150 for late spring and early
summer, 150-200 for winter)
First-aid kit
Avalanche transceivers and probes
Snow shovels
Snow saw
Repair kit (duct tape, two-part quick epoxy, needle and thread, utility knife
with basic tools to adjust all hardware, tent-pole repair supplies, stove
maintenance kit)
Altimeter
Cellular phone
GPS unit

SANITATION AND BLUE BAGS

Since so many people visit the upper slopes of Rainier, the disposal of human waste requires special attention. Cold temperatures and lack of soil limit the number and activity of microorganisms that normally break down human waste, and the feces remains. Not only is this aesthetically displeasing, but it also poses a serious health risk for climbers who gather snow from the area for water. Wind can also transport contaminated snow to clean areas.

Outhouses are provided at Camp Schurman and Camp Muir. At other locations on Mount Rainier, use the blue-bag system for human waste disposal. The system utilizes a pair of plastic bags; sets of the bags are issued free when climbers register. During your climb, defecate on the snow away from camp or route. Use the inner blue bag as a glove to pick up the waste. Turn the bag inside out; secure it closed with one of the twist ties that are provided, and deposit it in the second, larger bag. Then twist-tie this bag shut also. Urine should not be collected.

Carry the bag in your pack until it can be properly disposed of. Along the principal Paradise and White River climbing routes, bags can be deposited in one of the black collection barrels placed at central locations. In popular areas such as Emmons Flats and Ingraham Flats, deposit barrels have privacy screens. Use the privacy area as the bathroom, bag your waste, and drop it in the barrel. The barrels are flown off the mountain in the fall and the waste is incinerated.

If there are no barrels on your route, ask a ranger if there is a drop location near the trailhead. All fecal waste should be blue-bagged and then carried until it can be deposited in a black barrel (not in an outhouse).

WHEN TO CLIMB

Choosing the date of the climb will depend partly upon your goals. If your overriding interest is in reaching the summit, you will probably climb in the summer months, which offer the highest likelihood of success. Those looking for solitude, independent challenges, or a more rigorous mountaineering experience often climb during the off-season.

SPRING

Some of the best climbing conditions are found in April, May, and June. A great deal of winter snow remains on Mount Rainier's glaciers and rocky ridges, helping to minimize problems that get worse with the heat of summer: exposed icy sections, large crevasses, and loose, rotten rock. The mountain has a pristine, fresh appearance in spring, and you're more likely to have a classic mountaineering experience. Although you may see other climbers on popular routes, crowds and permit limits are less likely to be an issue.

The unpredictable factor during this time of year is weather. Spring storms are common, and unstable weather may persist for a week or more. Try to allow yourself as much as 7 days to climb the mountain in case the weather changes its mood.

SUMMER

July and August bring the highest summit success rates. Summer days are long and the weather is predictably better. And by that time, hundreds of preceding climbers have established the standard routes, kicking steps and placing route-marking wands. Summer storms may come, but they are generally short in duration and severity. Consider that summer climbing also means crowds on the popular routes and at high camps.

AUTUMN

September and October can offer excellent weather, but the days are shorter and the nights are colder. Winter snows, like the crowds of summer, have vanished by then, and the glaciers become hard and icy. Moderate ice climbing skills are needed due to the increased hazards of steep, icy terrain. You will also need good routefinding skills as the glaciers become broken, jumbled masses of crevasses and icefalls. The path to the summit will be circuitous.

Sudden storms can arise, and your ascent may quickly turn into a winter climb. If you're intent on reaching the summit, give yourself a week in order to allow for bad weather and difficult glacier navigation.

WINTER

Climbing Rainier in winter is truly one of North America's great mountaineering experiences. The mountain is beautifully covered in snow, the routes are more direct, and the crowds of summer are five months away. But be forewarned, climbing Rainier may also be your longest epic and the most grueling and defeating trip imaginable. Short days, fierce winds, cold temperatures, and deep snow all contribute to make standard routes extremely difficult and successful winter ascents a rarity.

Much of your success will depend upon the weather, but there are some things you can do to lessen the chance of your climb turning into an epic. Give yourself a minimum of one week, preferably in late February or March. The days are longer than earlier in winter, and a week should be enough time to give you a chance at the summit.

Snow bridges and crevasse crossings become more hazardous and exciting late in the summer. This climber negotiates the upper Emmons Glacier in September.

Get in good physical and mental shape. Actually, get in excellent shape. Winter climbs are hard on the body and demand exceptional endurance. Take cold-weather gear that you've tested and know will keep you comfortable. Assume that you will be rained, blown, snowed, and sunned upon. Carry a spare pair of gloves. Have a full set of insulating synthetic garments—pants, shirt, jacket—topped by a rain jacket and rain pants. Your sleeping bag can have either synthetic or down fill. Down works great, but remember that moisture and down are a bad combination, and down won't dry out on the mountain.

If it's raining while you're still in the parking lot, wait. Staying dry in the rain on Rainier is nearly impossible, and the weather rarely gets better as you ascend. If you do insist on going, remember that constant exposure to the severe trio of rain, snow, and wind is demoralizing and hard on your constitution. Teams that sit out big storms on the mountain are usually eager to go home when the weather breaks, not head for summit. But if the weather is good at the parking lot, GO!

A winter gear list should include a good supply of bamboo wands (150 to 200) to mark your route to high camp and above. The wands are placed on the ascent, then picked up again on the descent. Each person should also carry a snow shovel and avalanche transceiver—along with a knowledge of how to use them and how to recognize avalanche hazards. Depending on conditions, you will probably want snowshoes or skis for a portion of the climb to keep you from postholing through the deep snow. Mount Rainier is noted for heavy snowfall. For many years it held the world record for snowfall within one year at 1,122 inches, or 93 feet. A ski descent of at least part of your route can be an incredible experience. Crampons are required for areas where deep snow gives way to wind-scoured ice.

Think ahead about how you will establish your winter camp. Be prepared to set up your tent in a storm while your hands are freezing and you're hungry and tired. Secure the tent with wide stakes that can hold in snow, not the thin aluminum stakes that came with it. In addition, you can secure the tent with extra ice tools, ski poles, or shovels that are placed in the snow.

In cold weather, check the elastic shock cords that hold sections of tent poles together. The cords remain elongated when it's very cold, making it difficult to set up a tent because the elastic no longer pulls the poles together. You can retie the cords a few inches shorter or rewarm them in your jacket.

In selecting tent or bivy sites, figure out which way the wind has been blowing and build snow walls to protect camp. Or build a snow cave, if you've learned how. A snow cave can be a lifesaving refuge during a storm and is much more comfortable than a tent if you're confined inside for any length of time.

How well does your stove work on snow? Does it need a stand to prevent it from melting into the snow? Comforts such as spare socks become invaluable after a few days. Think carefully about what is critical for your success. Always carry a backup or materials for repair for any item you must not lose. A storm can pin a team down for a week or more. What happens if your stove fails or the tent blows out?

Winter climbers who leave from Paradise must park their vehicles in the lower lot by the Henry M. Jackson Visitor Center. This permits plows to remove new snowfall in the upper parking lot for daily traffic. (Vehicles parked overnight in the wrong place can get plowed in or buried with snow from the plows.)

During the late fall, winter, and spring, a gate at Longmire prevents uphill traffic toward Paradise at night and while snowplows are at work. It's not uncommon for the gate to remain closed till noon or later during large storms or when the avalanche danger is extreme. To avoid a long wait in Longmire, call ahead and ask when the road is scheduled to be open (360-569-2211, Ext. 2334). Have snow tires on your car and carry tire chains and a shovel. The Longmire Museum, the small building near the road gate, is the best place to get a climbing permit in fall, winter, and early spring.

DURATION OF THE CLIMB

If climbing Mount Rainier is a serious goal, don't limit the outing to 2 days, even in summer on a standard route. Be generous and allow extra days to make the most of the trip. The routine 2-day standard climb may seem attractive to people with limited time, but teams that spend several days on the mountain generally have the best experiences.

There are many advantages to a 3- or 4-day climb, the most obvious being versatility. Why limit the chance of success to 1 or 2 days after so much preparation? If something goes wrong, you'll have the additional time to recuperate and try again. Foul weather frequently denies the summit even to strong, well-prepared teams. An extra day or two could allow a second attempt.

Teams also could use an extra day to rest and acclimatize before the summit push. Many climbers reach the top of Rainier at such great effort that they are unable to enjoy the success. That extra day of rest and acclimatization can help a climber stand strong and healthy on the summit, rather than feeling wasted and sick while worrying about the trip down.

Extra days also make trips safer. Teams that spend an extra day at high camp, or take a half day to climb to an advanced high camp, are better prepared for the demands of a long summit day. A well-positioned and rested team moves more efficiently. Being swift and strong enables rope teams to move through hazardous areas rapidly, spending less time exposed to uncontrollable mountain variables such as rockfall or avalanches.

For many people, climbing Mount Rainier is an adventure they have planned and dreamed about for months, if not years. Building in an extra day or two will give you a chance to enjoy all aspects of the climb. It's a margin for both safety and enjoyment—a simple way to acknowledge that there's no good reason to hurry through the climb only to rush back to the parking lot, the highway, and the daily routine.

SAFETY AND SURVIVAL

This National Park Service warning sign was destroyed by weather. The message, however, remains truer than ever. © Eric Simonson

Climbing Mount Rainier can be deadly. This section of the book is dedicated to your safety and will address mountaineering hazards, how to avoid them, and what to do if you run into trouble. I've heard climbers dismiss warnings, claiming that their greatest danger lies in driving their car to the trailhead. Maybe, maybe not. Park Service statistics indicate that climbers are more likely than any other park visitors to be killed or seriously injured. The resources and technology exist to help make climbing safer, but the sport is inherently unsafe.

The objective dangers of mountaineering are evident. These are the hazards we have no control over: crevasses, avalanches, lightning, blizzards, high altitude, rockfall, and icefall. But you can learn to recognize these hazards and to reduce your exposure to them. (See the full discussion on avalanches, in a later section of the text.)

Subjective hazards—the ones we have some control over—are equally threatening. They include such negative factors as improper training, inadequate equipment, or poor conditioning. Is your team physically and mentally ready for the rigors of mountain climbing? Can you rely upon your teammates if you are in trouble? Do you know how to perform a self-rescue? What happens if someone becomes sick from the altitude?

The most dangerous element on the mountain is the human one: the climbers themselves. Poor planning and bad decisions contribute to virtually every mountaineering accident. Humans cause most of the avalanches that kill. Many lost or distressed climbers ignore the obvious signs of deteriorating weather. Frostbite, hypothermia, dehydration, mountain sickness, and other medical problems all have precursors and are conditions that can be reversed in the field. (See the detailed section on medical problems, in a later portion of the text.) Climbers have the ability to control many of the dangers that can become life-threatening emergencies. The importance of being independent and prepared for any situation cannot be stressed enough. Self-reliance during an emergency is critical to your chances of survival and may prevent small incidents from turning into huge problems.

AS THE WEATHER TURNS

Inclement weather on Mount Rainier is the biggest contributor to mountaineering problems. Every year, climbers are rescued or bodies are recovered because a combination of bad decisions and bad weather nailed them. (See the later separate section on weather for a full discussion of Mount Rainier weather patterns, season by season.)

Climbing teams on the way to the summit from high camp should carry a map and compass, plus bivouac gear and a snow shovel. If the weather begins to deteriorate, reassess the situation. What will happen if conditions worsen? Are team members prepared to spend the night high on the mountain? What will happen if the storm persists for days? It's certainly OK to continue climbing in poor weather, but teams who do so need to possess the resources to help themselves. It's irresponsible to leave the proper gear back at high camp, expecting a rescue if an emergency arises.

Placing wands to mark the route, using a map and compass, staying hydrated, and eating regularly may allow skilled and confident teams to reach the summit even under poor weather conditions. Teams that lack any of the essential equipment, water, or food should turn around in deteriorating weather—or expect the worst. Some experienced climbers choose to go extra light, leaving safety items behind in the interests of speed and reduced weight. This can be OK too, for teams with a lot of experience in the mountains. Seasoned climbers understand the severity of poor weather and usually elect to turn back. A disregard for the weather can lead to deadly accidents. Open a mountaineering accident journal, and this scenario will be found year after year, all over the world.

Whiteouts, blizzards, freezing rain, and high winds are conditions that most frequently trouble climbers on Rainier. It's difficult to negotiate technical terrain in these circumstances. Climbers become disoriented and are unable to recognize other mountaineering hazards, such as crevasses, icefalls, or increased avalanche risk.

In a whiteout, as fog and clouds move in, the terrain and atmosphere merge into one. The light is flat and even, making it impossible to distinguish features and slopes. Objects may appear to be in the distance but in reality be only one or two feet away. It even becomes difficult to tell up from down on the slope. When this happens, stop moving, dig in, and wait it out. Teams on a glacier should not attempt to navigate by map and compass, because these won't indicate crevasses. Whiteouts are the most common weather-related problem on Mount Rainier.

Thunderstorms with lightning occur every year, particularly on the north and east sides of the mountain. The most common result of these storms is lower-elevation forest fires, but lightning is also a serious danger for climbers, who carry a plethora of metal objects—some quite long and thin, resembling lightning rods. The hut at Camp Schurman has been struck by lightning, and so have climbers on the Muir Snowfield. The best defense is to avoid buildings and high places. When large thunderheads begin to build or approach the mountain, descend immediately. Climbers on the north and northeast sides are at a disadvantage when storms rapidly circle the mountain from the south and catch them by surprise. If this happens, find cover, possibly in a crevasse that can be walked into. Stay low so you don't become a conductor.

AVOIDING ACCIDENTS

The best way to avoid climbing accidents or to stop them before they cause serious injury is to become familiar with basic climbing techniques such as roped glacier travel, ice ax arrest, team rescue and self-rescue from crevasses, and crampon techniques. You can test your skills on smaller glaciated peaks such as Mount Baker, Mount Hood, or Mount Adams before attempting Rainier.

Even after earnest training, the risk of accidents is great. The environment poses challenges that demand constant attention. Accidents such as slips on steep snow or tripping on crampons are common. Be sure your crampon straps are tucked away and that your gaiters fit snugly. Keep crampons well-adjusted and tightly fitted to the boots. If they work loose, readjust them immediately in a safe location. Crampons ball up with snow during soft, wet conditions, so bang the snow out of the spikes with your ice ax. If conditions demand frequent banging, consider removing the crampons.

Most of the terrain on Mount Rainier is rated as moderate, but don't become complacent because the terrain lacks obvious technical difficulties or severe exposure. If a short slip isn't stopped immediately, the momentum quickly leads to a loss of control and a fast and dangerous slide down the slope. Practice self-arrest techniques individually and as a team, and make them second nature.

There will always be unavoidable hazards on Mount Rainier. Objective dangers such as rockfall, avalanches, crevasses, and icefalls can spell disaster for a team that is in the wrong place at the wrong time. Avalanches are dealt with in detail in a later section. Following are ways to limit your exposure to the dangers of rockfall, crevasses, and icefalls.

First of all, look with suspicion on any Rainier climbing route that involves exposure to rock. The rock on Rainier is volcanic—rotten and unstable. During cold periods, snow and ice help to hold the rock together. Warm weather and solar radiation melt the snow and ice, bringing a significant increase in rockfall hazard.

The best defense is to move quickly and to never take rest breaks in exposed locations. A helmet will afford protection from small falling rocks. In fact, a helmet is generally a good idea on Rainier, offering head protection during a crevasse fall and defense against any gear dropped by climbers above.

The glaciers on Mount Rainier are noted for large crevasses and for icefalls, those especially steep and chaotic sections of a glacier. These areas change dramatically from season to season. Winter and spring snowfall blankets crevasses and fills in icefalls. Summer heat melts this snow, and the glaciers become broken and crevasses become more noticeable. As late summer and fall arrive, the glaciers become dry and icy, with a majority of crevasses exposed.

Crevasses and icefalls are dangerous any time of year, and it's strongly recommended that climbers rope up on any glaciated terrain. Extra care is needed in winter and spring, when crevasses are hidden under unstable snow and climbers are in danger of falling through hidden holes and disappearing into a crevasse. Although crevasses become more apparent in the summer and thus are easier to avoid, there is still a danger of falling into them while crossing weakening snow bridges.

At the same time, icefalls begin to melt. As they do, large blocks of ice and snow tumble down the mountain, sometimes thousands of feet, destroying everything in their path. These large avalanches of ice seem to come at random, occurring both day and night, though activity is usually less during the colder periods. Later in the summer and early fall, glacier surfaces become hard and icy. Most of the snow bridges have melted out by then, and climbers must make an end run around crevasses. Icefalls are extremely broken, and climbing them would be time-consuming and dangerous.

Move quickly over snow bridges and under or through icefalls. As with rockfall hazard areas, don't stop for breaks; the less time in the danger zone, the better. Generally speaking, there is safety in speed if it is controlled. Climb when temperatures are below freezing, making the snow and ice more stable. In the summer, get an alpine start—getting under way well before dawn. On hard and icy terrain, move carefully and be sure your crampons are sharp and well-adjusted. Be aware that it's difficult to self-arrest on glacier ice.

On the descent of the mountain, it's safer to avoid seat glissading. Sprained ankles, broken femurs, dislocated kneecaps, and crevasse falls have resulted from what many climbers feel is an innocuous descent technique. It can be difficult to get a good view of the terrain below while glissading, and it's easy to catch a boot or crampon in the snow. In such a tumble, you can easily lose gear. It's usually smarter to simply walk down the mountain.

TEAM DYNAMICS

Rainier guide Eric Simonson put it well: "Safety isn't just knowing how *you're* doing, it's knowing how *everyone* is doing." At the same time that you pay close attention to your own climbing, watch for signs of problems within the team. If a member exhibits some continuing problem with the climb, stop to assess the situation and act to correct it.

Teams need to be able to recognize dangerous situations and take precautions to ensure the safety of all members. Belays and the placing of protection—such as ice screws or snow pickets—may be necessary to prevent crevasse falls or other slips that could result in catastrophe for the whole team. On the other hand, if the team decides to proceed without belays or protection, it may actually be safer to not rope up, so that the fall of one climber cannot result in the entire team careening down the mountain. This approach is usually taken on the Success Cleaver climb, for example.

Teams should stay together on the mountain, both on the ascent and descent. Some members of a party may be tempted to charge ahead of team-mates who are not moving as rapidly. But leaving part of a team behind can lead to trouble, particularly when someone is having difficulties or during de-teriorating weather. Teammates are responsible for each other until everyone is safely off the mountain and back at the car, and letting the selfish goals of a few supersede the needs of a team is dangerous. Teammates are the best re-source during an emergency, but once a party is split up, that resource is seri-ously compromised. The mission of a true team is to stick together, work through tough situations, and support one another.

RESCUES

No one plans to need rescue, but every year the Mount Rainier climbing rangers conduct numerous searches, rescues, or body recoveries. Volunteer mountain rescue units and the guide services are sometimes called on to assist.

Before a team seeks help in an emergency, such as a crevasse fall or illness or climbing injury, it needs to do everything possible to handle the situation by itself. This is where specialized training proves its value. The American Red Cross, climbing clubs, and community colleges are among organizations that may offer courses in cardiopulmonary resuscitation (CPR), mountaineering oriented first aid (MOFA), standard and advanced first aid, and emergency medical technician (EMT) training. With people on your team with such train-ing, you're ready to treat for shock, serious bleeding, airway obstruction, bro-ken bones, or spinal injuries, and for other medical emergencies.

If the crisis is beyond the ability of your team to handle, enlist the aid of any other parties that are nearby. Mountaineering etiquette asks that climb-ers assist each other in an emergency. In case the team still remains in seri-ous trouble, send a member for help or have another climbing party pass the word. If a cellular phone is available, give it a try. These phones perform with mixed results on the upper mountain. Determine before the climb which emer-gency phone numbers would be helpful to you, and bring the numbers with you. Call 911—but be aware that you may get a dispatcher in Yakima, Seattle, Tacoma, Ellensburg, or in some cases Oregon, who will then have to transfer

U.S. Army Chinooks assist National Park Service climbing rangers during many upper-mountain rescues. The double-rotor power and large carrying capacity of the Chinooks are perfect for transporting rescue teams to high elevations. Here, a long-line is used to remove the body of a climber who fell into a crevasse on the upper Emmons Glacier.

the call and information to the park. To reach the Park Service directly, call 360-569-2211, Ext. 2334. Save the phone's batteries for the emergency only. Rather than calling friends and relatives to inform them of the situation, reserve the phone for communicating with your rescuers.

Climbing rangers staff the high camps at Muir and Schurman during the summer. They have rescue gear, medical supplies, and Park Service radios. Climbers have access year-round to emergency radios inside the community hut at Muir and the hut at Schurman.

After the emergency is reported, a member of the team should keep a record of events. Record details such as how an illness or injury occurred, the patient's medical symptoms, duration of periods of unconsciousness, pulse and respiration rates, past medical history, medications used, and any other information that can assist diagnosis and care.

Continually reassess what can be done to facilitate the rescue. If a helicopter is called, try to get the victim to a large, flat area for pickup. Many routes lack such locations, but they do exist here and there. If the rescue involves carryout on a litter, have patience while rescuers are on the way. Continue to eat, drink, and stay warm. Keep the patient comfortable, and treat the illness or injury as best you can.

Ground rescuers will be moving under heavy packs, carrying medical supplies, climbing and rescue gear, extra food, and other equipment to aid in the emergency. A team awaiting help can sometimes assist by descending partway down the mountain to meet rescuers. The lower on the mountain you can safely go, the quicker the rescue can proceed and the sooner the patient will be in the hands of a doctor.

A team in trouble cannot automatically expect helicopter rescue. The Park Service launches a helicopter only when there is a life-threatening or limb-threatening emergency and when weather and other conditions safely permit. Otherwise, ground rescuers will most likely respond to the emergency and may take a day or more to reach the team, especially in a remote location or during poor weather.

The taxpayer gets the bill for virtually every rescue, since climbing fees do not pay for such operations on Mount Rainier. If a climbing team is found to be grossly negligent, it can be billed for the cost of its rescue.

WEATHER

The weather on Mount Rainier is as diverse and unforgiving as the terrain. Strong storms know no season; high winds, rain, snow, and subfreezing temperatures can occur any month of the year. Many mountaineering accidents are weather-related, and climbers always need to factor the season and weather into their plans. Keeping track of mountain weather can be critical to a safe climb.

Mount Rainier generates its own weather. Because of local variations in wind flow, lifting air, sinking air, and Rainier's great height, amazing changes in weather are common from day to day, hour to hour, and elevation to elevation. Cool temperatures, light winds, and foggy skies near Paradise may give way to clear skies only an hour's hike above on a typical summer day. And Rainier's weather can be extreme. When it's wet, it's damp and penetrating; when it's windy, it's cutting and fierce; and when it's cold, it's brutally frigid.

Prepare for the weather by watching changes and trends. Use the radio, television, or Internet to get tuned into the weather situation before the climb. Up-to-the-hour weather observations for Paradise on Mount Rainier are available in late fall, winter, and early spring at the Northwest Weather and Avalanche Center's Web site: www.nwac.noaa.gov. The site includes other useful information such as daily mountain weather and avalanche forecasts. You can find out if the weather has been cold and wet or warm and dry; if it has been windy or calm. This knowledge will help in selecting the appropriate equipment and gaining a good idea of what's ahead: deep snow, ice, wind, sun, cold, or whatever. The phone number for the Northwest Weather and Avalanche Center is 206-526-6677. Begin with a solid forecast and then observe and mentally record meteorological events from the beginning of the climb. Maintain a mental picture of what is happening with the weather. The best way to learn weather is to keep your eyes open. Use telltale clues to continually update your weather information and your personal weather forecast. Then use this knowledge to modify routes, camp locations, and summit climb preparations.

When on the mountain, use the common clues that indicate deteriorating weather. Early storm signs include cloud caps (lenticular clouds); increasing cirrus clouds from the west or southwest; a lowering barometer (rising altimeter); and changing or backing winds. Increasing winds and precipitation are obvious signs of changing weather. Monitor these clues throughout the climb.

The weather on Mount Rainier can be dramatically different from what it is elsewhere in Washington. The mountain and its 12,000 feet of vertical relief directly influence what's happening on the peak. For example, moist air from the Pacific cools by approximately 3.5 degrees Fahrenheit (2 degrees Celsius) for every 1,000 feet (roughly 300 meters) that it rises. This cooling produces temperature differences of 30 degrees Fahrenheit or more between Paradise at 5,420 feet and the summit at 14,410 feet.

As the moist air rises and cools, it condenses, producing precipitation and whiteout conditions. A good example of this is a lenticular cloud sitting on the upper mountain. While this rising air can greatly increase precipitation on the windward side of the mountain, the sinking air common on the lee side may help to minimize precipitation as it warms and dries. Therefore it's not uncommon to find clearer weather on the Winthrop and Emmons Glaciers on the northeast side of Mount Rainier.

Other local weather effects induced by the mountain include small-scale wind eddies and turbulent swirls—formed as winds interact with ridges, ribs, valleys, gullies, and rock outcroppings. Also, solar heating and radiant cooling produce substantial daily cycles of rising and falling mountain winds. During the clear nights and early-morning hours of summer, heat loss off the snow, rock, and ice creates a river of cold, dense air that flows down the mountain. Conversely, solar radiation warms air close to the surface during the day, producing an up-mountain wind during the late-morning and afternoon hours.

SPRING: APRIL TO EARLY JUNE

After months of harsh winter weather, storm cycles decrease their intensity as spring arrives. Storms are less frequent and less powerful in April and May. Breaks in the weather allow the sun to bring the year's first real warming to the mountain.

Spring storms are often followed by intense heating from the sun as days become longer. This causes a rapid warming and melting of snow as the air temperature at Paradise remains above freezing.

Spring days may seem like summer, but don't be deceived into thinking summer has arrived. During this transition in seasons, sudden and unexpected storms are still likely. April averages 10 inches of measurable precipitation and close to 70 inches of snowfall. Rain at Paradise means heavy snow on the mountain. Continue to watch for signs of approaching storms, and look for clues to a weakening snowpack and increased avalanche danger. Expect changing weather even during a pattern of apparent stability.

SUMMER: LATE JUNE TO EARLY SEPTEMBER

Summer weather provides the most stable opportunities for climbing. Good conditions make Rainier a popular summer climb.

Clear, warm weather is likely in late July, August, and early September. Even during the worst of years, Paradise has received only 6 inches of snowfall during August. Both July and September have recorded years of no measurable precipitation. A high-pressure ridge normally develops off Washington's coast during these months. It pushes storm energy to the north or splits and weakens its intensity offshore. It's not unusual for freezing levels to hover up at 12,000 to 14,000 feet as precipitation dwindles significantly.

June and early July are a bit more temperamental than late summer. Springlike storms that deposit significant snow are common. The effects of solar radiation are the greatest during the long days of June and early July, particularly on clean, bright, reflective snow. Such reflection makes cirques and bowls seem like ovens, even above 10,000 feet. This can lead to significant surface snowmelt and the dangers to climbers of wet loose avalanches, weakening snow bridges, rockfall and icefall, sunburn, snow-blindness, and dehydration.

Cold, clear nights result in radiant cooling of the snow. As the snow refreezes after the day's heat, a substantial crust is formed. This crust can make for good cramponing and climbing on crystal-clear days.

AUTUMN: MID-SEPTEMBER TO EARLY NOVEMBER

During late September and October, the jet stream begins to dip southward into the Pacific Northwest. The increased onshore flow associated with decreasing heat from the sun allows storms to bring a surge of prewinter conditions to the mountain. It's entirely possible to find a foot or two of snowfall at Paradise in September and October. But just as possible is the return of a summerlike high-pressure ridge, sometimes for a week or two. When this happens, expect brilliant clear days and cold nights, a so-called Indian summer.

With November and December approaching, the sun recedes lower on the horizon, producing a strong temperature contrast between the north and south poles. During this imbalance the onshore flow over the Pacific Northwest increases even more. Pacific-born storms now bring heavy rain, snow, ice,

Climbers battle fierce winds, even in the summer. Little Tahoma is in the background.

wind, and lowering freezing levels. Winter has started and climbers should be prepared for blizzard conditions.

WINTER: LATE NOVEMBER TO LATE MARCH

Winter on Mount Rainier generally means frequent clouds and heavy precipitation. Several major storms hit the mountain each winter. The storms produce heavy rain or substantial snowfall and high winds, particularly above treeline. Storms can last for a week or more and may deposit 80 to 100 inches of snow and bring temperatures below zero degrees Fahrenheit and winds in excess of 100 miles per hour. Anyone climbing in winter should be prepared for hostile conditions.

Due to Washington's temperate climate, it's not uncommon for the freezing level to rise above 9,000 feet in winter. During these periods, the avalanche hazard is greatly intensified and traveling on suspect slopes should be avoided.

Inevitably the freezing level will lower back to between 2,000 and 5,000 feet. Rain-soaked and windblown snow becomes stable, crusty, and icy, and pockets of wind-deposited snow fill the cracks of the glaciers, ridges, and rocks. The climbing can be very good at this time if significant snowfall doesn't follow immediately.

Climbers should be aware that storms will change the appearance of the landscape. Whiteouts severely impair visibility, making navigation much more difficult. High winds can slowly blow climbers off track, even when using a compass. Rime ice attaches itself to any exposed object, cloaking the appearance of rocks. A few hours of heavy snowfall and high winds will quickly form new cornices and rocks once visible may become buried. A boot track will vanish within 10 minutes. Recognize these added challenges of a winter storm.

Some winters experience a break in the westerly flow of storms. This happens when a large upper ridge of cold air flows over the Pacific Northwest, resulting in several days to a week or more of clear weather, especially at higher elevations. During this time, northeast and northwest winds commonly buffet the mountain.

As this high-pressure, cold-air ridge moves eastward over Washington, northerly winds yield to weak westerlies, increasing the high clouds in the sky and freezing levels on the mountain. The pressure gradient becomes great between the east and west side of the state, causing heavy cold air to sink under the warmer air aloft. Strong temperature inversions are likely between 4,000 and 6,000 feet, trapping low-level moisture as a blanket of low clouds or fog in the valleys.

As the pressure ridge continues east over the Cascades, south and south-west winds increase and return. This change breaks the inversion, mixing the moist surface air with drier air aloft. This turnover is often abrupt, resulting in dramatic changes in the weather and in the stability of the snowpack. The storm clock is ticking. During such air-mass transitions, extreme weather is likely and avalanches are certain. Winter weather returns as heavy precipitation and high winds again prevail.

AVALANCHES

Mount Rainier is home to vast areas of classic avalanche terrain, with long, moderately steep slopes and massive annual accumulations of new snow. The mountain also sees thousands of enthusiastic climbers each year—many of them ignorant of the conditions that create and trigger the avalanches that could end their climb in tragedy.

Avalanche awareness is mandatory for safe travel on Mount Rainier. With such a wide variety of weather, terrain, and snowpack, avalanche hazard is likely somewhere on the mountain much of the year. Climbers should understand what causes avalanches, know how to assess conditions, and be prepared to rescue an avalanche victim.

The best approach is to learn to avoid being caught in an avalanche in the first place. But if you are swept away and buried, your best chance lies in a fast, efficient rescue from your teammates. In any venture onto potentially dangerous avalanche terrain, every climber should carry an avalanche rescue beacon, and know how to use it. Teams also need to carry strong snow shovels and avalanche probe poles.

TYPES OF AVALANCHES

There are two distinct types of avalanches: loose and slab. They can be wet or dry, hard or soft.

Loose avalanches (loose slides; also sometimes called point-release avalanches) begin at a single point and gradually entrain more snow as they fan out, forming an inverted V-shape. Such slides are usually initiated by single snow grains that exceed their angle of repose, sliding downhill and bumping into neighboring snow grains as gravity takes over. Loose slides are frequent on steep, smooth slopes or cliff areas. Some loose slides are relatively small and harmless—simple sluffs. But others can grow large, even triggering dangerous slab slides as they descend. Even a moderate loose slide can be deadly if it carries an unwary climber into a terrain trap like a crevasse, or over a cliff.

Slab avalanches occur when cohesion between snow grains allows entire layers of snow on a slope to give way at once. For a slab avalanche, all that is needed is the slab itself, a poor attachment of the slab to the layer below, and the sliding surface. A significant danger arises when buried weak layers of snow are unable to support the overlying snow as it constantly creeps downhill and adds stress. The area of weakness may be small, or it may be widespread enough to cause an entire slope to fracture and release.

A variety of conditions can trigger slab avalanches. Changing weather may be the most common factor. This includes heavy snowfall or a rapid change (normally a rise) in air temperature. Rain can also be a prime instigator, adding weight without strength to the snowpack while weakening the surface snow and increasing its downslope motion. Other triggers include loose avalanches, rockfall and icefall, falling cornices and, most notably, climbers postholing through the snow. Regardless of the trigger, slab avalanches are deadly. It's not uncommon for them to become huge—sometimes incorporating several layers of snow from past storms, and in some cases the entire winter snowpack.

WEATHER, TERRAIN, AND THE SNOWPACK

Conditions for an avalanche are created by a combination of weather, terrain, and the snowpack. The weather interacts with the terrain to produce the snowpack. Then the weather and terrain continue to interact with the snowpack, constantly altering its characteristics and stability.

SNOWPACK AND WEATHER

Constant variations in the weather can occur as snow falls. Changes in temperature, in wind speed and direction, and in precipitation type and rate cause snow to accumulate in a wide variety of layers—some weak, some strong; some thick, some thin. The bonds between these layers may range from rock solid to shaky. The vertical relationship of these layers largely determines the stability of the snow. Overall, stronger layers (higher-density snow) deposited over weaker layers (lower-density snow) produce less stability.

Increases in temperature, wind speed, or rate of precipitation often lead to an increasingly unstable snowpack. Rising temperatures with snowfall result in dense, heavy snow being deposited over weaker, lighter snow. Increasing winds produce higher-density, wind-slab snow over less cohesive and weaker snow. And high snowfall rates do not allow buried weak layers and newly deposited snow time to settle and stabilize. All of these scenarios can create an unstable snowpack that loads and stresses weak layers to the point of failure.

Snow-crystal shapes also affect stability of the snow. Small, simple snow crystals generally produce more slab-like snow than larger more intricate

A small avalanche can quickly turn large and disastrous, as this one did in the upper Nisqually Basin, near Nisqually Cleaver. This slide released shortly after the morning sun hit the snow slope above.

snowflakes do. But high winds can break intricate crystals into smaller shapes, which make a more cohesive slab layer. Snow pellets (graupel) are an extreme example of crystals that contribute to instability; they often form a cohesionless layer in the snowpack. Hoar frost or surface hoar, the ice equivalent of dew, can also affect slope stability; if buried intact, this thin and notoriously weak crystal layer frequently produces avalanching.

SNOWPACK AND TERRAIN

There is great variability in what can be considered avalanche terrain, from large, steep snow bowls to minor chutes and open faces. Most slides occur in well-defined paths with a starting zone, a running track, and a runout or deposition area. Avalanche terrain exists almost anywhere there is an unstable slab on a steep enough slope to slide. On Mount Rainier, this means much of the upper mountain.

Even during days of high avalanche hazard, however, careful routefinding can guide you to relatively safe avenues. Minimize your time in avalanche terrain by selecting a route subject to less hazard. Often the safest routes are along the crests of ribs or ridges, especially when they are windswept. Take into account, though, whether shifting winds could transport snow that loads both sides of the ridge or creates unstable cornices.

Cross any potential avalanche slope as high as possible, one person at a time. Move quickly from anchor point to anchor point (exposed rocks and other safe areas), each person using the same track. In most cases, being caught near the top of a slide is better than being in the middle or bottom, where all the snow above can bury you.

Recognizing slope angles is a critical part of assessing avalanche danger. Slab avalanches are most common on slope angles between 30 and 45 degrees. Large slides from steeply angled slopes are less likely because frequent smaller slides reduce the stresses and the amount of snow. Slope angles below 30 degrees tend to compress and stabilize, though they too can slide if a particularly weak layer exists below. Be aware of even relatively minor changes in slope angle. The transition from 30 to 35 degrees may not seem like a big change to you, but to the snowpack it may mean the difference between stability and avalanche release.

RATING THE DANGERS

In analyzing avalanche danger, consider the three primary factors: weather, terrain, and snowpack. Rate the current conditions of each as a red (danger), yellow (caution), or green (safe). If any one of the three factors comes up as a red, stop and take a very close look at the other two.

If current snowpack conditions, for example, are clearly in the red—very unstable snow, with cracking or evidence of recent avalanches—make sure you've got a good, safe green for the terrain (you'll be traveling through flat areas or up on windswept ridges) and for the weather (temperatures are dropping and there's no wind). But if terrain or weather conditions are verging on yellow or red, change your route or come back another day.

Thinking about the three factors and their changing contributions to stability as red, yellow, or green lights is a very effective way to remain avalanche aware.

Learning avalanche awareness is as important as learning how to use an ice ax or crampons, especially on Rainier. The Northwest Avalanche Institute offers avalanche evaluation and forecasting courses that specialize in conditions in the Pacific Northwest and on Mount Rainier (39238 258th Avenue SE, Enumclaw, WA 98022; 360-825-9261; www.avalanche.org/~nai).

During late fall, winter, and early spring, mountain weather and avalanche forecast information is provided by the Northwest Weather and Avalanche Center. Information is available on the Internet at www.nwac.noaa.gov or by calling 206-526-6677.

HEALTH

This was the first of our eighteen summit climbs that season as climbing rangers for Mount Rainier. We had pulled over the top of the Kautz Headwall and were suddenly struggling against an invisible force. Our pace slacked off as we hauled ourselves up the last 300 feet to the summit. As I congratulated my partner, he suddenly bent over and vomited. This veteran of twenty-four Rainier summits looked up with a smile and said, "Every year on the first summit of the season I lose my stomach and get wasted, but I recover quickly while descending. After a few weeks acclimatization, it'll be a different world up here."

The climb of Mount Rainier is unusual for North American mountains in that nonacclimatized climbers routinely travel from their home at sea level to a trailhead at 5,000 feet and on to the summit at 14,410 feet in less than 48 hours. This is a greater altitude gain than the trip from base camp to the summit of Denali (Mount McKinley) that takes most climbers 10 to 14 days. This rapid gain in altitude—the invisible force that hit me and my partner on our way up Rainier—requires special attention because it endangers our performance and safety significantly.

HIGH-ALTITUDE ILLNESSES

Above 8,000 feet, any gain in altitude forces our bodies to contend with a significantly lower level of oxygen in our bloodstream. The summit of Rainier has a third less oxygen than sea level as a result of the lower atmospheric pressure. If we were willing to be patient enough to achieve the same gain in altitude by gradual ascent over a week or more, our bodies would have time to adjust, and we would perform much better. Ultimately a climber's only protection from the effects of a rapid ascent of Rainier is to descend before these effects of altitude progress to life-threatening illness. On a typical ascent of Mount Rainier without prior acclimatization, we are racing the clock.

Altitude illness commonly shows up as mild symptoms of acute mountain sickness (AMS), including headache, malaise, lassitude, poor appetite, nausea, vomiting, dizziness, and irritability. Nearly 70 percent of climbers on Rainier suffer from acute mountain sickness during their summit climb.

Acute mountain sickness is not life-threatening, but ignoring it is. The illness may worsen, over hours or days, as dangerous collections of fluid develop in the lungs and/or the brain. Significant fluid in the lungs (high altitude pulmonary edema, or HAPE) results in shortness of breath while at rest and a further reduction of oxygen transfer to the body. Increasing fluid in the brain (high altitude cerebral edema, or HACE) causes loss of balance, confusion, and hallucination. If descent or oxygen supplementation is not accomplished within hours, coma and death may ensue.

HOW TO AVOID ALTITUDE ILLNESS

Gradual ascent of Mount Rainier over several days reduces the likelihood of acute mountain sickness because your body has time to adapt. Only rarely do climbers have this luxury of time, however. Most climbers simply accept the symptoms of AMS during a summit climb as part of the overall experience.

It's possible to help prevent the symptoms of AMS with the use of simple drugs like acetazolamide (250 milligrams twice a day or 500 milligrams slow-release once a day) or aspirin (325 milligrams three times a day) at the start of the climb. Acetazolamide is particularly useful in improving poor sleep at high altitude. However, these medicines do not protect against the development of serious altitude illness: high altitude pulmonary edema and high altitude cerebral edema.

Some non-drug measures can decrease the symptoms of high-altitude illness and help performance. They include the following.

- Begin a high-carbohydrate diet one or two days before the climb.
- Make climbing plans that take into account your decreased work capacity at high altitude.
- Reschedule the climb if you come down with an upper respiratory or other active infection.
- Avoid overexertion on the climb by maintaining a reasonable pace and not overloading yourself with nonessential gear.
- Drink enough fluids on the climb to offset increased fluid loss. Passing urine that is clear is a good sign that you're drinking enough fluids.
- Provide good ventilation for camp stoves used in confined places.

SYMPTOMS AND TREATMENT

The critical point about altitude illness is to not let acute mountain sickness progress to life-threatening HAPE or HACE. It's not uncommon for climbers to dismiss their symptoms as other maladies and push on. If anyone in your party is experiencing even mild symptoms, do not ascend farther to sleep at a higher camp. If the symptoms are worsening, the person should descend. Do not let your team member descend alone. The decision to descend must be made well before the patient loses the ability to walk down.

An actual incident illustrates how early symptoms of altitude illness can proceed to something far worse. A small research team ascended over 3 days to camp in Rainier's summit crater. One member of the group had developed AMS at a previous camp but attributed his malady to overexertion. The climber's condition worsened that evening, and he could not help in establishing camp on the summit due to the illness, which now included shortness of breath at rest and poor balance.

At sunset, the team leader alerted climbing rangers, who were also on the summit. They found the patient in his tent, disoriented and unable to support himself. Descent at night with a physically impaired climber would have been too dangerous. Shortly thereafter, the patient became unconscious and required assisted breathing intermittently. Climbing rangers from Camp Muir attempted to carry up oxygen but were unsuccessful due to poor weather. The patient was still alive at dawn, when the weather improved enough to permit a helicopter evacuation from the summit. The climber, suffering from severe AMS and HACE, recovered fully in a hospital.

The red-flag symptoms that indicate the need for **immediate descent** include shortness of breath at rest; the coughing up of pink, frothy sputum; poor balance; confusion; or a decreased level of consciousness. Descent must not be delayed if any one of these signs is present. The seriousness of these signs cannot be overstated. Without descent or supplemental oxygen, death may occur within hours. Waiting for a rescue, without some form of supplemental oxygen, is a desperate option.

Medications may help with severe altitude illness, but only rarely do they make a critical difference and thus they cannot be relied on. Each has benefits, but they can also cause harm if not used correctly. They include the following drugs.

Acetazolamide is very safe, and is used to treat acute mountain sickness, high altitude pulmonary edema, and high altitude cerebral edema. Take 250 milligrams twice a day or 500 milligrams slow-release once a day. It must not be taken by people with a known intolerance to sulfa drugs.

Dexamethasone is safe when used for treatment of HACE while descending. It may also be used to treat patients with HAPE if you suspect HACE may also be present. The dosage is 4 milligrams every six hours. The drug is dangerous if given as an aid to ascent.

In addition to high-altitude illnesses, any number of other medical emergencies can occur during a Rainier climb. The sustained strenuous climbing can precipitate a variety of medical problems. If you have a condition that limits your activity at home or that is managed with medications, check with your doctor before venturing high on Rainier. During the climb, descent can only help with any medical condition that develops at high altitude. When in doubt, descend.

COLD-WEATHER HAZARDS

The cold temperatures encountered during a Mount Rainier climb can have serious health consequences. Climbers can learn to guard against hypothermia and frostbite and to treat the conditions if they occur.

HYPOTHERMIA

Hypothermia is a drop in the core body temperature to below 95 degrees Fahrenheit (35 degrees Celsius). Hypothermia can occur rapidly after a sudden event like immersion in cold water or a radical change in weather. It can also develop slowly if the body's metabolism isn't adequate to meet ongoing environmental exposure.

Hypothermia occurs both ways on Mount Rainier. A person who falls into a crevasse while lightly dressed for a sunny midafternoon glacier crossing will be at risk if not extricated quickly. More slowly but just as surely, hypothermia can affect a climber who has eaten little food while climbing through the day with a heavy pack, leaving the body with lessened ability to produce heat as the sun drops and the wind kicks up. Most deaths from this slow form of hypothermia occur at relatively mild temperatures, between 30 degrees and 50 degrees Fahrenheit (-1 degree to 10 degrees Celsius). You can die of hypothermia in the summer.

Prevention is a matter of minimizing excessive heat loss and ensuring adequate heat production. This is achieved through

- proper choice and use of clothing and shelter.
- staying dry.
- adequate nutrition and hydration.
- avoidance of overexertion.
- preparation for sudden changes in the conditions of the climb.

Hypothermia is progressive. Symptoms of mild hypothermia include a loss of judgment and of fine-motor coordination. The patient shivers to keep warm. This is readily reversible in the field. Patients can warm themselves once they are protected from further heat loss and are given rapidly absorbed high-energy food. A reasonable initial maneuver is for the patient to huddle with other members of the party behind some form of wind barrier, gaining warmth from the teammates. Early recognition and treatment of mild hypothermia may avoid the progression to profound hypothermia.

As profound hypothermia sets in, shivering ceases and the patient becomes confused, with loss of coordination progressing to apathy, stupor, and coma. People with profound hypothermia cannot warm themselves. Provide the patient with wind protection, remove wet clothing, and apply prewarmed insulation (including a ground layer) to prevent additional heat loss. It's essential to provide warming by applying heat packs or hot water bottles next to the patient's body; cuddling with the patient inside a sleeping bag or bivy sack also is effective. Begin these procedures as soon as possible. If the patient is in a stupor or unconscious, use gentle handling to avoid triggering an irregular heart beat. Never assume that the patient has died; continue the rewarming process.

FROSTBITE

Frostbite is a localized area of frozen tissue. It occurs most commonly at the end of extremities and uncovered areas during exposure to subfreezing temperatures. The risk of frostbite increases with extreme cold, high winds, high altitude, dehydration, and overexertion. Wearing tight clothing or footwear, or using alcohol, tobacco, or other drugs, also increases the risk. Especially vulnerable are parts of the body that are in contact with metals or liquids or that have been frostbitten in the past.

Superficial frostbite results in pale, cold skin with underlying tissue that is pliable and soft. Treat with skin-to-skin contact or by immersion in water that is just warm to the touch of the caregiver's elbow (104 to 108 degrees Fahrenheit). If the frostbite produces blisters, the patient should be evacuated to receive further treatment. If the frostbite is on the foot, the patient shouldn't try to walk.

Deep frostbite involves the skin and deep structures that become hard and nonpliable. The decision to thaw deep frostbite depends on the situation. Rewarming requires both proper technique to minimize tissue damage and use of a strong painkiller or narcotic. To prevent further damage, don't use the affected part after thawing. Thawing in the field usually isn't called for on Mount Rainier, however, because rapid evacuation can often be organized.

Corneal frostbite is rare but can occur in extreme cold and high winds. Irreversible damage may occur, requiring a corneal transplant. If you travel in such harsh conditions, wear goggles and cover exposed skin.

OTHER MEDICAL CONCERNS

Mount Rainier can confront climbers with any number of other medical problems.

HEAT SICKNESS, EXHAUSTION, AND DEHYDRATION

These conditions can disable even a strong, fit climber. They are common on Mount Rainier, where climbers face frequent and rapid extreme changes in weather conditions during a sustained period of physical activity. The conditions result from a lack of attention to basic nutrition, hydration, and regulation of body heat by adjusting clothing layers. Each of these ailments points to its own cure. Heat sickness (dangerous overheating) requires urgent rapid cooling. Exhaustion warrants rest and high-energy food. Dehydration and electrolyte imbalance requires the drinking of water containing salts and sugar.

The symptoms of these conditions overlap with those of altitude illness. Sorting out these potentially dangerous conditions can be difficult. Carefully evaluate a patient's symptoms and closely follow the responses to initial therapy, while maintaining a suspicion that altitude sickness is involved. More than one illness may be occurring at the same time.

SNOW-BLINDNESS AND SUNBURN

These conditions are surprisingly common on Mount Rainier despite well-known preventive measures. Both snow-blindness and sunburn result from direct tissue irritation by the ultraviolet (UV) rays of sunlight. The UV dose is dependent on the intensity and duration of exposure to sunlight, which increases with altitude. Although both ailments may occur throughout the year, they are more common in the sun-intense spring and summer, especially on snow-covered slopes.

For sunburn, barrier methods are very effective, such as light clothing to cover extremities. Apply sunscreen (SPF 15 or higher) or zinc oxide paste frequently to sun-exposed areas when you are perspiring.

High-quality sunglasses filter out most UV light, and combined with side shields they offer extremely effective eye protection. Cheap sunglasses can actually increase the risk of snow-blindness because they do not filter out a significant proportion of the UV rays but still permit pupils to dilate.

ON THE MOUNTAIN

The first part of a Rainier climb is the journey from trailhead to high camp, a trek that can take anywhere from 3 hours to 2 days depending on the climbing route you've chosen. In some cases, the trip to high camp can be longer and more arduous than the summit climb itself. Leave early to maximize the use of daylight hours. Problems such as blisters, equipment troubles, or struggling teammates may arise on the way. Arriving at base camp early allows extra time to set up, prepare, and rest. Drink and eat at regular intervals on the hike to camp and after you get there. Keeping fluid and energy levels high will help you acclimatize and perform better.

On the way to high camp, you'll pass through different ecological zones, the most fragile of which are the subalpine and alpine zones between 5,000 and 11,000 feet in elevation. What may appear to be bare ground can actually be home to small plant colonies thousands of years old. Stay on the trails; if there are none, simply watch your footing and try not to crush alpine plants, which rely on the short summer season for growth and reproduction. Unfortunately the meadows and fields above Paradise show signs of distress, with random trails and shortcuts causing erosion and plant damage.

HIGH CAMPS AND BIVOUACS

High camps vary greatly on Mount Rainier. You may find yourself in the crowded community shelter at Camp Muir or alone on the Tahoma Glacier, at popular Camp Schurman or at a bivy site on the Kautz Glacier route. In choosing a tent location, look for an area that offers protection from the weather and from objective hazards. Avoid sites that expose you to high winds, lightning, rockfall, or avalanche terrain. On a glacier, probe the site to ensure you haven't pitched your tent above a crevasse. Camp on snow whenever possible to avoid damage to vegetation; snow walls can be built to help protect camp and offer privacy. Never build new rock walls, windbreaks, or tent platforms on bare ground because they kill vegetation, cause erosion, and leave scars that last for decades.

Camp Muir, at an elevation of 10,080 feet, qualifies as a small community with its A-frame ranger hut, guide/cook shack, client hut, three outhouses, and 75-year-old public shelter. Use of the stone shelter, which can sleep up to thirty people on two long bunk platforms, is on a first-come, first-served

A climber fords Tahoma Creek on the approach to Tahoma Cleaver. Fording creeks and crossing glacial moraines are some of the challenges that face climbers on the way to high camp.

basis. Climbers who can't find room in the shelter or who prefer not to stay there set up camp on the snow outside.

The Muir shelter is spartan, but it provides great protection during stormy weather. Be forewarned: The shelter is not for light sleepers. It is every bit a climbers' shack, with more snoring, smelly, restless climbers than you ever thought you'd spend a night with at 10,000 feet. The shelter is equipped with a park-frequency radio for emergency use. Naturally it's important that every climber who stays here cleans up his or her own mess and never leaves a thing. Leftover food only attracts mice, and any other abandoned items simply add to the clutter.

The only structures at Camp Schurman are the ranger hut and an outhouse. Climbing rangers staff the hut in summer. During an emergency when no rangers are there, climbers can enter the hut and use the two-way radio that is kept behind the door.

At most high camps, you'll have to melt snow for drinking water. Get rid of contamination by using water filters or iodine tablets, or by boiling the water for 1 minute.

EVENING ON THE MOUNTAIN

Climbing camps are generally social places, and it's common to find other teams with similar summit plans or climbing experiences. Here you may find future climbing partners, advice both good and bad, or a piece to that broken stove. Returning teams may have recent route information or stories to share. Don't be afraid to ask around if you have questions or need help.

At the same time, privacy and solitude are pleasures that some climbers seek. Climbers can respect each other's space and the wilderness experience by not camping too close together and by keeping noise and voice levels low. Sound carries extremely well on those quiet mountain evenings, and few people enjoy a neighbor's music, singing, yodeling, or conversation while looking for peace and quiet. I've heard all sorts of musical instruments on the mountain, and most climbers agree that the sound of a harmonica is no more appealing at 10,000 feet than at sea level if you're trying to get some sleep. Early risers can also help by keeping noise levels down for the benefit of parties opting for a later start.

At best, however, it may be difficult to get a good night's sleep before summit day. Hit the sack early to maximize rest; a few hours of sleep before the climb will help immensely. Climbers who think it's easier to skip sleep and head toward the summit after sunset often hit a wall after a few thousand feet.

Most people have no problem sleeping after the hard climb to high camp, but others may find that excitement and anxiety keep them awake. Avoid napping before bedtime. When it's time to get into your sleeping bag, make yourself as comfortable as possible, and remember that lying horizontal is restful to the body even if you're unable to sleep. Try earplugs to help block noise from wind, other climbers, or your snoring tent partner. Doctors who specialize in high-altitude medicine recommend against use of sleeping pills, which reduce the breathing rate and may contribute to acute mountain sickness.

Before going to bed, complete all the final preparations for summit day. Get ropes and climbing gear ready, and double-check essential gear such as crampons, headlamps, and backpacks. Make the final decisions about your rope teams. Most rope teams put the leader in front, the second-most experienced climber in the back, and the least-experienced climber or climbers in the middle. Other teams choose rope order depending on fitness level, with the best pacesetter in front and the rope leader in the back. Consider the best scenario for your team and stick to it.

SUMMIT DAY

The planning and preparation all come down to this one day. This is when you may discover that all your careful work does not necessarily guarantee success. You may go to bed on a star-filled night, feeling good, and waken to a headache and a stormy day. Or you could go to sleep during a storm, only

Summit day high on Liberty Ridge. The clouds remain stable below.
© *George Beilstein*

to find excellent climbing conditions when you arise. If your body and the mountain both cooperate, you'll soon be heading toward the summit.

Prepare for a long day. Most teams need between 6 to 10 hours to reach the summit from high camp and another 3 to 5 hours for the return trip to high camp. A predawn departure—an alpine start—is the norm in order to make the most of the day and to ascend and descend in the cooler hours when snow and ice are more stable.

WHAT TO BRING

Mountaineers differ on what should be carried in a summit pack. The most conservative plan is to carry all your gear from high camp so you'll have everything you need in case you get stuck for an extended period on the mountain. Climbers every year get pinned down high on the mountain by storms, injury, or illness. On the other hand, a lighter pack feels better and allows you to move more quickly. If you go light, consider the consequences of stormy weather or an accident. Will you be able to help yourself and your teammates, regardless of the proximity of other parties or of rescue rangers? Carry the items you feel will be necessary in an emergency. Weigh the virtues of a heavier pack versus a light rucksack. Both have their advantages, and on any given day one may be preferable to the other. The decision is yours.

Recommended team gear during a summit climb includes a snow shovel, stove with pot and fuel, insulating pad, bivy sack, first-aid kit, wands, repair kit for crampons and other essential items, and gear for belays and crevasse rescue. Personal essentials on a summit climb include a headlamp with extra batteries and bulb, food, two quarts of water, warm jacket, sunglasses, sunscreen, map and compass, matches, knife, and personal medication. Think about your summit climb and ask, "What will I need to safely continue climbing if conditions degenerate?"

WHEN AND WHAT TO EAT

Your body will perform better if it's adequately hydrated and fueled from the start, so give yourself the advantage of drinking and eating before leaving on the climb. A food rich in carbohydrates, along with a quart of water, makes for a good pre-climb breakfast.

Excitement, anxiety, high altitude, and other factors can commonly make the prospect of food unappealing. If this is the case for you after you arise on summit day, at least try snacking on a candy bar or energy bar and having something to drink. But don't make yourself sick by forcing something down. If you feel OK, start the climb anyway and try eating during the breaks. Hopefully you'll regain your appetite as you move up the mountain.

Continue to eat and drink every hour or two during the climb. Bring food you enjoy, but don't indulge in a lot of sugary snacks that may leave you feeling empty later. Precooked red potatoes, yams, and sweet potatoes are good food items on summit day. Keep some food easily accessible for short rest breaks.

PACE AND BREAKS

Set a good pace from the start. There's a fine line between too slow and too fast. A good pace allows climbers to breathe rhythmically, think clearly, and get up the mountain in a timely fashion. If you're struggling to maintain your footing, to keep your crampons off the rope, and to stay up with your teammates, you probably won't be able to continue for long. If you trained properly, a steady pace with breathing at every step will take you to the summit. Communicate with your rope leader about the pace. Try for a rhythm that team members can maintain for an elevation gain of 1,000 to 1,500 feet before requiring a break. Climb steadily. It's not a race; steady upward movement is what counts.

Most people feel good for the first 1,000 to 2,000 feet of elevation gain above

Continuing to keep a good pace becomes important late in the climb. Here, climbers keep their heads down and push as they approach the bergschrund near 13,600 feet. For many, the last few hundred feet of elevation gain are the hardest.

high camp. A few will quickly realize they're in over their head and opt to stop or turn back, while some others will make it even higher and then call it quits. The breaking point for most teams is around 12,500 to 13,500 feet—after 5 to 6 hours on the standard routes. The effects of altitude and physical exhaustion really kick in. That great pace you set may pull you through, but be prepared for the psychological battles as you try to continue when your body is screaming to stop. Even the best athletes slow near the summit. Don't be discouraged. Fortitude has pulled many people up the last thousand feet.

There is no doctrine on when or how long you should rest during the ascent. Breaking more than once an hour, however, will significantly slow the team down. Stop only in safe locations, avoiding areas of crevasse, rockfall, or icefall hazard. If your team must stop in an exposed location, anchor the climbing rope and secure your pack and any other loose items that may blow away or slide down the mountain. Use breaks to eat, drink, check your gear, take pictures, and discuss plans. If you need to defecate, step off the climbing route and make use of a blue bag, but stay tied in to a rope. Pack the blue bag with you, and deposit it later in one of the barrels at the popular high camps or in a trailhead collection barrel.

PASSING

On a busy route, don't be surprised to find yourself passing other parties or having other parties pass you. Rope teams passing each other as they climb can be a hazardous and stressful operation. If possible, pass while the other party is taking a break. As in backpacking, it's considered polite to allow faster teams to pass. Stepping off route for a minute or two will allow a faster party to pass safely without cutting you off.

Fast or impatient teams may try to pass if they're stuck behind a slower party. I've witnessed many arguments over who should go first and who is faster—confrontations and "horse races" that tire team members. Let impatient parties pass. And if your group would like to pass another rope team, talk with the last person on the rope ahead and ask if you can get by. This usually works. If you still can't get around the slower team, it's time to try a little patience: Focus on your surroundings and take in the view. Soon enough, you'll find a safe way to move ahead.

THE SUMMIT AND CRATER

You may believe you're home free once you see the rocks along the summit crater rim, but many climbers feel that this only marks the hardest part

A climber enjoys the sunset from Columbia Crest. The lights of Puget Sound cities illuminate the horizon.

of the climb. Keep your head down and stay with your pace. Soon you'll reach the rim and enter the crater.

Most parties reach the crater rim at a point where they can seek protection from the elements. Parties generally unrope and take a break here. You're now at the summit—almost. You'll still need to walk a quarter-mile across the flat floor of the small crater if you want to stand on Columbia Crest. This highest point, at 14,410 feet, is a small snowy knoll on the west rim of the crater. With the air considerably thinner at 14,000 feet than at sea level, tired climbers often find this walk through the crater a lot more difficult than it appears.

From Columbia Crest on a clear day, you can see for a hundred miles in any direction. The summit plateau is so broad, however—more than a mile across—that Rainier's shoulders obscure lower parts of the mountain and other peaks within the park.

If the weather is particularly nice and you're feeling well, there are many things to explore while on the summit. The summit plateau has two other notable high points: Liberty Cap, at 14,112 feet, to the northwest, and Point Success, at 14,158 feet, to the southwest. Both can be a pleasant stroll for climbers who are still in good shape. The two points appear close by, but don't be deceived. It usually takes 1½ to 2 hours for the round trip from Columbia Crest to Liberty Cap, and about an hour for a similar round-trip hike to Point Success. Point Success is on a narrow ridge that offers a unique view of Rainier's south side, including the Tahoma Glacier and Paradise. Liberty Cap is a snowy point that quickly rolls away to the precipitous north and west flanks of Rainier.

You can also explore the steam caves created in the summit crater by hot volcanic gases within the mountain. Numerous fumaroles (vents) let gases escape through the soft mud and rock under the snowcap. From inside the crater, you can sometimes see steam venting in small clouds. The crater entrances to the caves change throughout the year depending on snowfall, but the passages themselves remain more or less the same. The network of tunnels is extensive, and scientists have mapped them over the years.

Some of the tunnels are small and require visitors to crawl. Others are large and cavernous. One tunnel houses the remains of a small airplane that crashed on the summit in 1990 and melted through the ice; it now resides in a mangled heap on the cavern floor. It's even possible for knowledgeable explorers to enter the caves at one point and cross beneath the crater snowcap, exiting a quarter-mile away on the opposite side by linking the correct tunnels. Visitors to the caves can expect to get wet from the steam and muddy from the volcanic clay. The caves are a unique feature that have provided shelter for many

Caves and tunnels lace much of the crater's rim. Here, a scientist collects high-altitude water samples from the grotto lake 150 feet below the summit crater ice cap.

climbers caught on the summit, including Hazard Stevens and Philemon Beecher Van Trump during the mountain's first documented ascent, in 1870.

Sleeping is another popular pastime in the crater. But keep an eye on the time. Those rare days when skies are clear and winds are calm can quickly change, and I've found the summit to be most typically a place where you prepare for your descent.

DESCENDING

Going down the mountain can be as physically demanding and dangerous as going up. Acute mountain sickness, fatigue, hunger, and other problems can make it difficult to stay focused for a safe descent. A majority of mountaineering accidents occur during the descent, and parties need to take extra care to avoid mistakes that can lead to accidents.

On the standard routes, most teams need 3 to 5 hours for a safe descent to high camp. Before leaving the summit, check critical equipment such as crampons, ropes, and harnesses. Knots or crampon straps may have loosened during the climb. Tie back in to the climbing rope, and check with your teammates to ensure everyone is ready and nothing is left behind. Most teams put the most experienced or strongest climber last on the rope for the descent. If anyone falls, this person can respond quickly both as an anchor and leader.

Going downhill is aerobically easier than climbing up—you don't have to breathe as hard—but it's tougher on the body. Again, pace is important. The leader should set a pace that everyone can follow without tripping or without stepping on the rope. Continue periodic eating and drinking to stave off dehydration in the sun and to keep your body well fueled.

Try to get back to high camp before the afternoon heat weakens snow bridges and increases rockfall and icefall. The snow often becomes sticky and soft in the sun. Crampons collect soft snow between the spikes, making it difficult to gain traction. Banging them with your ice ax will remove the snow temporarily; some climbers remove their crampons if the snow is particularly stubborn. Generally it's safer to leave them on, however, in case you run into icy sections. Avoid the temptation to glissade on the upper mountain, which can lead to uncontrolled slides, injuries, or falls into crevasses.

Back at high camp, relax and refuel before heading down to the trailhead. If you're at one of the popular high camps, deposit any blue bags you have into the collection barrels. Again inspect your gear and clothing for damage. Go through camp and check that your team left no trace of its presence, picking up all trash, gear, and leftover food. Then it's a trek back to the trailhead. Check out at the ranger station, and your summit climb of Mount Rainier is history.

HOW TO USE THIS GUIDEBOOK

The thirty-nine principal climbing routes described in this guidebook are organized into four main sections, based on the area where climbers will leave the trailhead. These main sections are Paradise; Longmire and the Westside Road; Mowich Lake and Carbon River; and the White River area.

From each of these general starting areas, the routes are categorized by nearby prominent features and place names on the mountain. For instance, the Longmire/Westside approaches allow access to three prominent mountain features—Success Cleaver, Tahoma Cleaver, and Puyallup Cleaver—which encompass eight distinct summit routes. (Cleavers are the prominent ridges that separate adjoining glaciers.)

Distances are given in miles, and elevations are listed in feet. To easily convert miles to kilometers, multiply by 1.6. To convert feet to meters, divide by 3.3.

THE ROUTE DESCRIPTIONS

Every route description begins with a short discussion of the route's particular qualities and features. This includes aesthetic value, views, points of interest, and other bits of information that help create a mental picture of what the route is like. Each description then provides entries with the following information.

Elevation gain: From the trailhead to the principal high point at the top of the route: Columbia Crest (elevation 14,410 feet), Point Success (elevation 14,158 feet), or Liberty Cap (elevation 14,112 feet). For the walk from Point Success to Columbia Crest, allow about half an hour. For the walk from Liberty Cap to Columbia Crest, allow about 45 minutes to 1½ hours.The listed elevation gain does not include the ups and downs in elevation that may be part of the overall ascent.

What to expect: Information on rockfall and other hazards, slope steepness, additional climbing factors, and the route's grade rating.

Time: Estimated number of days for a successful ascent and descent during favorable weather and climbing conditions. Also included are hour estimates for teams to ascend or descend the route between high camp and the summit. These estimates are generous and are based on consistent observations of independent climbers. Consider that larger teams move more slowly at high altitude, especially when they are roped together or include inexperienced climbers. Teams that have previously climbed together and are comfortable with the terrain and altitude can subtract a few hours here and there.

Season: The usual best months to climb that particular route. These recommendations consider the seasons, snow cover, access, and generally recognized optimum time and conditions to climb. The actual climatic conditions at the time of the climb will determine much of a route's difficulty.

First ascent: The climbers and the year of the original ascent and major variations.

High camp: Suggested camp for each route. Although bivouac options exist, the camps listed are generally the best and most direct for that particular climb. Exceptional bivy sites also are noted.

The full climbing descriptions are supported by detailed photo and written information about approaches, high camps, ascents, and descents. Many routes require glacier navigation. Glaciers change constantly and so do the routes. In these situations, the most common route is described. However, any glacier navigation may require extra routefinding skills as conditions change.

HOW THESE ROUTES WERE SELECTED

The routes for this guidebook were chosen based on popularity, usage trends, name recognition, and realistic climbing value. Some climbers contend Mount Rainier may have as many as eighty routes. While this is arguable, in reality only about seventeen routes are regularly attempted from year to year. This guide includes thirty-nine routes and numerous variations, though some are rarely climbed. These include the logical lines mountaineers take as they ascend the peak and are based on prominent geological features.

If the routes on Mount Rainier were categorized by every little chute, approach, couloir, ice runnel, rock band, face, or other feature, you might come up with a thousand routes and variations. If you consider that only a few feet may separate distinct routes at major sport-climbing venues like Smith Rock in Oregon, imagine the number of potential routes Rainier would provide.

CHOOSING YOUR ROUTE

Many climbers have heard of a few well-known routes on Mount Rainier and will choose to climb one of them based on name recognition. A great way to discover a route is through firsthand information and recommendations from reliable climbers and friends. If none of the routes are known to you, consider the mountain as a place to explore. Read about the routes here and then choose one that suits your goals, skills, and resources.

New climbers should consider one of the popular standard routes and allow a few extra days to give plenty of time for the approach to high camp, mountaineering practice, and becoming accustomed to mountain life. The Ingraham Direct/Disappointment Cleaver route and the Emmons Glacier route are the most-climbed on the mountain. They offer relatively good access to high camps and glaciers where teams can practice climbing skills. Professional guide services also use these routes. However, don't become lulled into a false sense of security by the presence of so many other climbers.

If solitude, independence, and getting off the beaten track are among your goals, look to routes on the west side of the mountain or climb in the fall, winter, or early spring. Teams that are ready to hike through forest, scramble up and down moraines, break trail, negotiate glaciers, and find their own way

Many climbing routes on the west side start below 3,000 feet and climb through temperate old-growth forest.

will enjoy routes that depart from Longmire, the Westside Road, or Mowich Lake. Many of these routes go without ascents year after year. And if teams are looking for something daring, seasoned mountaineers can test their skills on the challenging Grade IV and V routes. These routes are rarely climbed.

THE GRADING SYSTEM

The difficulty of mountaineering routes is measured in Roman numeral grades from I to VI, with I the easiest and VI the most difficult. Most climbers are familiar with the class ratings of rock climbing, such as a 5.10 rock climb or a class 3 scramble. These ratings measure the difficulty of the hardest move. Mountaineering grades are determined by the overall difficulty of the entire climb. Factors that contribute to the grade selection include elevation gain, duration of the climb, altitude, number of pitches, objective hazards, weather, level of commitment, and physical difficulty.

Snow, ice, and glacier climbs are challenging to grade. The technical difficulties of this type of climbing change with the weather, season, and year, making it difficult to give a climb a specific rating. The changeable current conditions are as critical as the more permanent known hazards of the route. Liberty Ridge, for example, typically has a steep, exposed, icy pitch near 13,000 feet; however, late-season climbers claim the hardest part of the route is crossing the Carbon Glacier to approach the ridge.

Grade I climbs may have any number of challenges, but the route can usually be completed in half a day or less, providing a quick escape and low commitment level. Rainier does not have any summit routes rated Grade I. Grades II and III involve more time on the route, perhaps a full day for the summit portion, plus some technical climbing. Many routes on Mount Rainier are Grade II or III because of their strenuous nature, altitude gain, steep terrain, glaciers, and level of commitment. Grade IV ascents include a full day of technical climbing, with pitches that require belays and with routefinding difficulties. Grade V routes demand 1 to 2 days of hard climbing involving difficult rock and ice-climbing moves. Grade VI routes call for difficult free-climbing on rock (5.10 and above), aid climbing, and ice climbing over 2 days; no routes on Rainier are rated Grade VI.

Grade II climbs may include the Emmons Glacier, Disappointment Cleaver, Gibraltar Ledges, Success Cleaver, and Kautz Cleaver routes. Grade III climbs include Liberty Ridge, Sunset Ridge, Nisqually Ice Cliff, and Nisqually Cleaver. Grade IV climbs include Ptarmigan Ridge, Curtis Ridge, Willis Wall, and Tahoma Cleaver. Routes that can be Grade V include the North Mowich Headwall and the Central Rib of Willis Wall. These climbs change with conditions. There may be a steep, icy section that becomes rock or mud as the season progresses. A straightforward climb in May could become very difficult by late August. Expect some surprises.

A NOTE ABOUT SAFETY

Safety is an important concern in all outdoor activities. No guidebook can alert you to every hazard or anticipate the limitations of every reader. Therefore, the descriptions of roads, trails, routes, and natural features in this book are not representations that a particular place or excursion will be safe for your party. When you follow any of the routes described in this book, you assume responsibility for your own safety. Under normal conditions, such excursions require the usual attention to traffic, road and trail conditions, weather, terrain, the capabilities of your party, and other factors. Keeping informed on current conditions and exercising common sense are the keys to a safe, enjoyable outing.

The Mountaineers

LEGEND

——— Climbing route

------- Major variation

▲ Camp (permanent or temporary)

● Land features

① Route number referred to in list

Facing page: Crevasses and climbers, Emmons Glacier

PART II

the routes

The Routes	Grade	Elev. Gain	Days
Paradise Approaches			
CAMP MUIR ROUTES			
Ingraham Glacier Direct	II	9,000	2–3
Disappointment Cleaver	II	9,000	2–3
Gibraltar Ledges (Gib Ledges)	II	9,000	2–3
Gibraltar Chute (Gib Chute)	II	9,000	2–3
Nisqually Ice Cliff	III	9,000	2–3
Nisqually Cleaver	III	9,000	2–3
Nisqually Icefall	II–III	9,000	2–3
WAPOWETY CLEAVER AND KAUTZ ROUTES			
Fuhrer Finger	II	9,000	2–4
Fuhrer Thumb	II	9,000	2–4
Wilson Glacier Headwall	II–III	9,000	2–4
Kautz Glacier	II–III	9,000	2–4
Kautz Headwall	III	9,000	2–4
Kautz Cleaver	II	9,000	2–4
Longmire and Westside Road Approaches			
SUCCESS CLEAVER ROUTES			
Success Couloirs	II	11,400	2–4
Success Cleaver	II	11,400	2–4
South Tahoma Headwall	III	11,400	2–4
TAHOMA CLEAVER ROUTE			
Tahoma Cleaver	III–IV	11,400	2–3
PUYALLUP CLEAVER ROUTES			
Tahoma Glacier	II	11,500	2–4
Tahoma Sickle	II	11,500	2–4
Sunset Amphitheater Ice Cap	III	11,400	2–4
Sunset Amphitheater Headwall Couloir	III	11,400	2–4
Sunset Ridge	III	11,400	2–4
Mowich Lake and Carbon River Approaches			
MOWICH FACE ROUTES			
Edmunds Headwall	III	9,200	2–3
Central Mowich Face	III–IV	9,200	2–4
North Mowich Headwall	IV	9,200	2–4
North Mowich Icefall	IV	9,200	2–4
PTARMIGAN RIDGE ROUTES			
Ptarmigan Ridge	IV	9,200	2–4
Ptarmigan Ice Cliff	IV	9,200	2–4
White River Approaches			
LOWER CURTIS RIDGE ROUTES			
Liberty Wall, Ice Cap	IV	9,700/11,800	2–5
Liberty Wall, Direct	IV	9,700/11,800	2–5
Liberty Ridge	III–IV	9,700/11,800	2–4
Willis Wall: Thermogenesis	III–IV	9,700/11,800	3–5
Willis Wall: West Rib	IV–V	9,700/11,800	3–5
Willis Wall: Central Rib	IV–V	9,700/11,800	3–5
Willis Wall: East Rib	IV–V	9,700/11,800	3–5
Willis Wall: East Willis Wall	IV	9,700/11,800	3–5
Curtis Ridge	IV	9,700/11,800	3–5
CAMP SCHURMAN ROUTES			
Winthrop Glacier/Russell Cliffs	II–III	10,000	2–3
Emmons/Winthrop Glaciers	II	10,000	2–3

PARADISE APPROACHES

Thirteen climbing routes encompass most of Mount Rainier's south side and can all be accessed from the Paradise area.

These climbs are categorized by proximity to Camp Muir, Wapowety Cleaver, or the Kautz Glacier area.

Camp Muir routes
Ingraham Glacier Direct
Disappointment Cleaver
Gibraltar Ledges (Gib Ledges)
Gibraltar Chute (Gib Chute)
Nisqually Ice Cliff
Nisqually Cleaver
Nisqually Icefall

Wapowety Cleaver routes
Fuhrer Finger
Fuhrer Thumb
Wilson Glacier Headwall

Kautz routes
Kautz Glacier
Kautz Headwall
Kautz Cleaver

Paradise is the major destination for most visitors coming to Mount Rainier National Park. There you'll find the Henry M. Jackson Visitor Center (the large, distinctive round building), Paradise Ranger Station, the guide service building, and Paradise Inn. Register and secure your climbing permit at the ranger station, at the upper end of the upper parking lot. If the ranger station is closed and the Jackson Visitor Center is open, get your permit there; it's a quarter-mile back down the road.

CAMP MUIR ROUTES

Seven climbing routes are best accessed from Camp Muir and the upper Muir Snowfield. Camp Muir has Rainier's shortest high-camp approach, and the climb from Paradise to Muir is one of the most popular in the park. Most parties take 4 to 8 hours to climb the 4,500 feet of elevation gain to Muir. Even the lower part of the route is often covered in snow till mid-June, but the trail to Pebble Creek at 7,200 feet melts out by midsummer. Near the start of the trail, climbers pass through Paradise Meadows, one of the park's most popular

Paradise Approaches
1. Ingraham Glacier/
   Disappointment Cleaver
2. Gibraltar Ledges
3. Gibraltar Chute
4. Nisqually Ice Cliff
5. Nisqually Cleaver
6. Nisqually Icefall
7. Fuhrer Finger
8. Fuhrer Thumb
9. Wilson Headwall

10. Kautz Glacier
11. Kautz Headwall
12. Kautz Cleaver

Emmons Glacier

Cowlitz Glacier

Cadaver Gap

Camp Muir

Gibraltar Rock

9,800 ft

Muir Snowfield

To Paradise

Nisqually Cleaver

Nisqually Glacier

Nisqually Glacier

Point Success

Kautz Glacier

Wilson Glacier

9,200 ft

Camp Hazard
11,300 ft

Kautz Headwall

Success Cleaver

Kautz Cleaver

visitor attractions. Expect hundreds of day hikers and sightseers in summer.

Getting to Camp Muir: From the Paradise upper parking lot (5,420 feet), take the Skyline Trail 1.5 miles to Panorama Point (6,900 feet). In summer, follow the trail to Pebble Creek (7,200 feet), where Muir Snowfield begins. When this section is heavily snow-covered, continue along the broad ridge above Panorama Point, staying west of McClure Rock (7,385 feet) to Muir Snowfield.

Once on Muir Snowfield, ascend north-northwest to Camp Muir at 10,080 feet. Along the way, climbers get dramatic views of Mount Adams, Mount St. Helens, Mount Hood, and sometimes even Mount Jefferson in central Oregon. The snowfield occasionally gets small crevasses in late summer, and the terrain is deceiving and difficult to navigate without the aid of a compass during storms and whiteouts. A map that includes compass bearings between Paradise and Camp Muir is available from the Park Service; you can ask for one when you get your permit.

Camp Muir has a ranger hut, guide/cook shack, client hut, outhouses, a public shelter, and tent camping areas near the shelter. The shelter building can accommodate thirty climbers overnight. An emergency radio is kept inside. The shelter is open year-round, but during the winter and spring the door is frequently blocked with spindrift snow that accumulates after storms, and climbers should then expect to dig for an hour to get in.

Ingraham Glacier Direct and Disappointment Cleaver

These routes, the most popular on Mount Rainier, see more than 6,000 climbers attempting the summit every year. These mountaineering classics begin where teams leave Camp Muir and cross the Cowlitz Glacier to Cathedral Rocks, a volcanic rock ridge, and then move onto the Ingraham Glacier. The route offers great views of Little Tahoma and Gibraltar Rock as teams ascend the steeper sections of the Ingraham Glacier or Disappointment Cleaver to access the upper mountain. The final push onto the upper Ingraham and Emmons Glaciers leaves the smaller peaks of the Cascade Mountains behind as Glacier Peak and Mount Stuart in the north come into view and the crater rim and summit are reached.

Although these routes are rewarding to climb, their popularity leads to heavy use and crowds. Do not expect a wilderness experience. There will be other climbers, and possibly even lines at tight locations along the route. Rainier Mountaineering Inc. leads more than 3,000 climbers up the DC—Disappointment Cleaver—every year. The guides do an excellent job ensuring that the route remains climbable throughout the summer—digging out

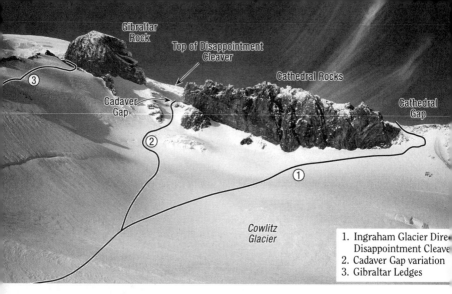

Gibraltar Rock

Top of Disappointment Cleaver

Cathedral Rocks

③

Cadaver Gap

Cathedral Gap

②

①

Cowlitz Glacier

1. Ingraham Glacier Direc
   Disappointment Cleave
2. Cadaver Gap variation
3. Gibraltar Ledges

the route, fixing hundreds of feet of rope, and sometimes even carrying ladders high onto the mountain to bridge small crevasses. Teams that leave Camp Muir late and fall behind a guided team should not become frustrated. Consider the route and its popularity, and enjoy the view.

ELEVATION GAIN: 9,000 feet from Paradise to Columbia Crest.

WHAT TO EXPECT: Rockfall and icefall hazards; 35- to 45-degree snow and ice slopes. Grade II.

TIME: 2 to 3 days; 6 to 8 hours from high camp to summit, 3 to 4 hours for descent to high camp.

SEASON: May through September.

FIRST ASCENT: Uncertain; possibly Allison L. Brown and six or seven Yakama Indians in 1885 or 1886.

HIGH CAMP: Camp Muir (10,080 feet) or Ingraham Flats (11,100 feet).

From Camp Muir, traverse the Cowlitz Glacier to Cathedral Gap (10,640 feet) and continue left along scree, frozen rock, and ice (snow-covered in early season) to Ingraham Glacier and to Ingraham Flats at 11,100 feet. The Ingraham Flats glacier camp enjoys dramatic summer sunrises and is a great high camp for teams wanting a shorter summit day. Climbers must use the blue-bag disposal system at Ingraham Flats.

An option for the route from Camp Muir to Ingraham Flats is to climb through the higher pass in Cathedral Rocks called Cadaver Gap. From Camp Muir, ascend north-northwest up the Cowlitz Glacier, skirting the bergschrund to the 11,250-foot gap, arriving just above Ingraham Flats. This variation has a reputation for avalanche and is a bit steeper than going over Cathedral Gap, but some climbers prefer it for its directness.

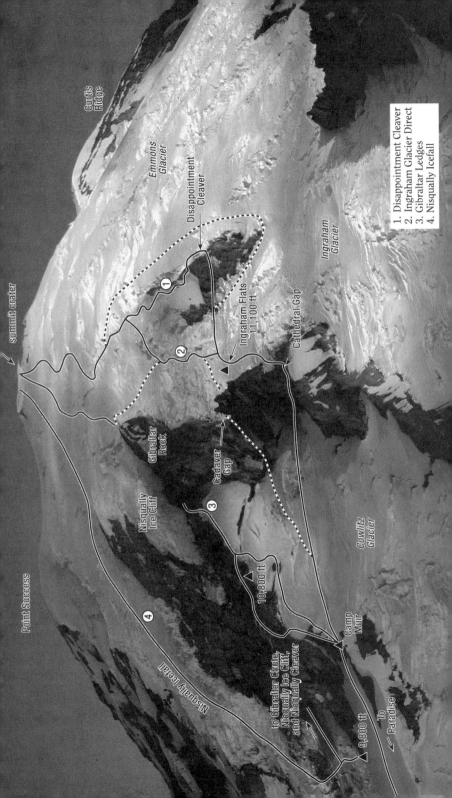

Curtis Ridge

Emmons Glacier

Disappointment Cleaver

summit crater

Ingraham Glacier

Ingraham Flats 11,100 ft

Cathedral Gap

Point Success

Gibraltar Rock

Cadaver Gap

Cowlitz Glacier

Nisqually Ice Cliff

10,800 ft

Camp Muir

to Gibraltar Chute, Nisqually Ice Cliff, and Nisqually Cleaver

Nisqually Icefall

9,800 ft

To Paradise

1. Disappointment Cleaver
2. Ingraham Glacier Direct
3. Gibraltar Ledges
4. Nisqually Icefall

From Ingraham Flats, there are two principal routes: the Ingraham Glacier Direct and Disappointment Cleaver.

In the early season, most climbers prefer the **Ingraham Direct route** because it is shorter and is less exposed to avalanches than the entrance and nose of Disappointment Cleaver. From Ingraham Flats, ascend westerly to the Ingraham Icefall. Move rapidly in the lower section of the icefall to avoid falling blocks, which occasionally cut loose and sweep parts of the route. Once in the icefall, continue up 25- to 30-degree slopes as you weave around crevasses and seracs to connect with the top of Disappointment Cleaver (12,250 feet). Occasionally, parties will climb to the left, or southerly, side of the glacier and connect with the top of Gibraltar Rock (12,600 feet), ascending slopes as steep as 50 degrees.

The **Disappointment Cleaver route** becomes more popular in June and July as the Ingraham Direct melts out and crevasse navigation becomes problematic. From Ingraham Flats, head westerly to gain the cleaver on a ledge system of crumbling rock 300 feet above the Flats. Move quickly and watch for icefall from seracs on the Ingraham Glacier while accessing the lower cleaver. Once on the cleaver, be extra conscientious of other parties. This is a bad area for passing other rope teams, and is noted for its high rockfall potential. The boots and ropes of other climbers loosen rocks, as do the warmer temperatures later in the day. The lower section of the cleaver is steep—30 to 45 degrees—and switchbacks up rock or southerly exposed snow slopes as it climbs to gentler terrain. Eventually the route reaches the top of the cleaver at 12,250 feet, a good rest spot.

The Ingraham Direct and Disappointment Cleaver routes join here at the top of the cleaver. Ascend the Ingraham and Emmons Glaciers to the summit on 25- to 30-degree slopes, negotiating crevasses and unstable snow bridges along the way. Climbers who choose to ascend from Ingraham Flats to the top of Gibraltar Rock will find similar conditions on the way to the summit. The routes reach the crater rim at 14,150 feet. From there it's about a 20-minute walk to Columbia Crest, the true summit, at 14,410 feet.

Descent: Descend the route you climbed. Move quickly in dangerous areas, and plan rest breaks for safe locations. The late-morning and afternoon heat weakens snow bridges and greatly intensifies rockfall hazard.

Gibraltar Ledges (Gib Ledges)

The Gibraltar Ledges provided the original summit route, first climbed by Hazard Stevens and Philemon Beecher Van Trump, in 1870. Now regarded as the standard winter route, it is also one of my personal favorites on Rainier.

The climb ascends from Camp Muir up the Cowlitz Cleaver, a rocky ridge dividing the Cowlitz and Nisqually Glaciers. This ridge affords great views of the Nisqually Glacier, Ice Cliff, and Icefall, which provide a showcase of avalanches and icefalls that can be safely observed from the route. Once at Gibraltar Rock, one of the most visible mountain features from Paradise, this classic mountaineering route follows a narrow and exposed ledge system of challenging and steep climbing to the high glaciers and upper mountain. The route should be traveled in colder conditions and preferably before the sun hits the south face and loosens rocks above the ledge.

ELEVATION GAIN: 9,000 feet from Paradise to Columbia Crest.

WHAT TO EXPECT: Serious rockfall hazard; 35- to 50-degree snow and ice slopes. Grade II.

TIME: 2 to 3 days; 6 to 8 hours from high camp to summit, 3 to 4 hours for descent to high camp.

SEASON: December through June.

FIRST ASCENT: First recorded ascent was by Hazard Stevens and Philemon Beecher Van Trump; August 17, 1870.

HIGH CAMP: Camp Muir (10,080 feet) or the Beehive (10,800 feet).

From Camp Muir, ascend the Cowlitz Cleaver or the left side of the Cowlitz Glacier to the base of Gibraltar Rock at 11,600 feet. You will pass the well-protected and excellent bivy sites at the Beehive (10,800 feet) while ascending the 25- to

A climber ascends Gibraltar Ledges before it connects with the upper Gibraltar Chute. Mount St. Helens is in the background.

45-degree slopes. If you climb the glacier, be aware of possible crevasses and bergschrunds.

Once you reach the base of Gibraltar Rock—at a spot sometimes called Camp Misery, not a recommended bivy site—find the obvious ledge that leads out to the left side (west side) of Gibraltar. This ledge system is usually covered with snow or ice, but may become rocky and melted out in June and July. It is strongly recommended that climbers wear helmets and move quickly while ascending the ledges. Gibraltar is notorious for rockfall, particularly on warm days.

Traverse and ascend the ledges (do not rappel or downclimb!) to Gib Chute, a 40- to 50- degree frozen snow or ice slope that leads to the top of Gibraltar Rock, 12,600 feet. This location is also known as Camp Comfort. However, climbers should avoid camping here as the site is exposed and thus offers little protection. Ascend the upper Nisqually and Ingraham Glaciers from Camp Comfort to the crater rim (14,150 feet), negotiating crevasses and unstable snow bridges along the way. From the rim, it's about a 20-minute walk to Columbia Crest, the true summit, at 14,410 feet.

Descent: Descend this route or the Ingraham Direct or Disappointment Cleaver routes.

Gibraltar Chute (Gib Chute)

To ascend Gibraltar Chute and three neighboring routes—Nisqually Ice Cliff, Nisqually Cleaver, and Nisqually Icefall—climbers enter the upper Nisqually

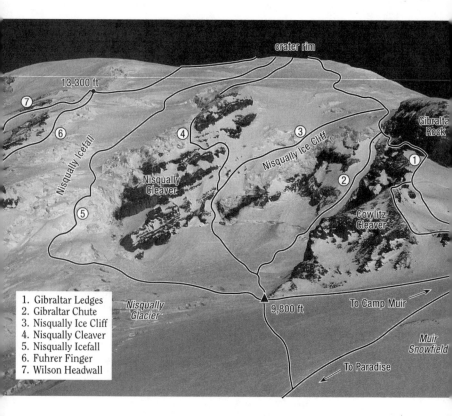

1. Gibraltar Ledges
2. Gibraltar Chute
3. Nisqually Ice Cliff
4. Nisqually Cleaver
5. Nisqually Icefall
6. Fuhrer Finger
7. Wilson Headwall

Basin, a fabulously wild cirque that is noted for frequent avalanches and ice-falls from the upper glacier and ice cliff. The car-size blocks of rock and ice that litter the glacier attest to this activity.

For these climbs, teams often camp at the base of the Cowlitz Cleaver (9,800 feet) on the edge of the Nisqually Glacier, a 5-minute walk from Camp Muir. The camp at the base of the cleaver offers excellent views of the routes, including any avalanche activity. Staying overnight here can be a humbling experience as avalanches roar off the upper Nisqually and send clouds of light snow through the camp.

Since Gib Chute and the three neighboring routes have substantial objective hazards, it is strongly recommended that climbers have high-level skills and the ability to move fast on steep technical terrain. Try to use a safer route for the descent; good choices include the Ingraham Direct, Disappointment Cleaver, and Gibraltar Ledges.

Gib Chute is arguably the most direct route to the summit. This prominent snow chute (or rock chute, in late season) lies between and below the Nisqually Ice Cliff and Gibraltar Rock. Although perfect for rapid ascents due to its directness, the route also exposes climbers to substantial rockfall and icefall from the Ice Cliff and Gibraltar Rock. Climbers must be prepared to accept a certain amount of risk.

ELEVATION GAIN: 9,000 feet from Paradise to Columbia Crest.

WHAT TO EXPECT: Substantial exposure to rockfall and icefall; 35- to 50-degree snow and ice slopes. Grade II.

TIME: 2 to 3 days; 6 to 8 hours from high camp to summit, 3 to 4 hours for descent to high camp.

SEASON: December through June.

FIRST ASCENT: Paul Gilbreath, Stan de Bruler, and a climber named Hewitt; July 1946.

HIGH CAMP: At the base of the Cowlitz Cleaver, just below Camp Muir, on the edge of the Nisqually Glacier (9,800 feet); or at Camp Muir (10,080 feet).

From the base of Cowlitz Cleaver (9,800 feet), head northwest out onto the Nisqually Glacier, climbing the right-hand side toward the chute, which is below the Nisqually Ice Cliff. Continue up the glacier toward the base of the chute; beware of rockfall from Gibraltar Ledges above. There may be a bergschrund to cross as you leave the glacier and head up the chute.

The route becomes gradually steeper as you ascend 1,200 feet to the narrowest point, or hourglass, below the Ice Cliff, where the angle reaches 45 degrees. Move quickly through this section, which particularly exposes climbers to rockfall and icefall. The slope angle increases to 50 degrees after the chute, but ascends under less stressful and hazardous conditions to the top of Gibraltar Rock (Camp Comfort). The chute may have sections of hard ice if icefall activity has recently scoured the route.

From Camp Comfort, ascend the upper Nisqually and Ingraham Glaciers to the crater rim (14,150 feet), negotiating crevasses and unstable snow bridges along the way. From the rim, it's about a 20-minute walk to Columbia Crest, the true summit, at 14,410 feet.

Descent: Descend the Ingraham Direct, Disappointment Cleaver, or Gibraltar Ledges back to high camp.

Nisqually Ice Cliff and Nisqually Cleaver

Deep winter snowpack and quick access from Paradise make these routes excellent winter and spring climbs. The upper Nisqually Basin, a glacier war zone of avalanches and icefalls, is crossed to access the steep ice slopes that ascend the Ice Cliff and the Cleaver. On the routes, climbers must negotiate crevasses, seracs, ice cliffs, and rock bands amidst uniquely beautiful glacier chaos. A speedy ascent is demanded for safety. Once the technical pitches are completed, the slope decreases and the routes move on to gentle glacier terrain. Late-season climbs are discouraged as these routes become too crevassed and the ice cliffs above avalanche frequently.

For additional general information related to these routes, see the introduction to the Gibraltar Chute route.

ELEVATION GAIN: 9,000 feet from Paradise to Columbia Crest.

WHAT TO EXPECT: Substantial exposure to rockfall and icefall; 35- to 60-degree snow and ice slopes. Grade III.

TIME: 2 to 3 days; 6 to 9 hours from high camp to summit, 3 to 4 hours for descent to high camp.

SEASON: December through June.

FIRST ASCENT: Nisqually Ice Cliff—Barry Bishop and Luther Jerstad; August 13, 1962. Nisqually Cleaver—Fred Dunham and James Wickwire; June 19, 1967.

HIGH CAMP: At the base of the Cowlitz Cleaver, just below Camp Muir, on the edge of the Nisqually Glacier (9,800 feet); or at Camp Muir (10,080 feet).

From the base of Cowlitz Cleaver (9,800 feet), head northwest onto the Nisqually Glacier, climbing to a large snow ramp that provides access to the lower left-

Leaving camp at 9,800 feet (base of Cowlitz Cleaver heading onto the Nisqually Glacier

hand side of the Nisqually Ice Cliff. There is a high objective hazard as you traverse and climb the Nisqually. Move quickly to avoid avalanches and ice blocks that liberate themselves from above and litter the glacier. Access the ramp by crossing the bergschrund, which is typically filled with debris from snowslides above. Climb the 55-degree ramp to a rock band directly overhead and a little to the right. This gains access to the shelf that forms the ice cliff itself. The ramp is at its steepest just below the rock band. Traverse and climb right, along the ice shelf. The ice cliff and cleaver routes separate at about 11,400 feet, shortly after the rock band.

To ascend the **Nisqually Ice Cliff route**, ascend right (east) along the top of the ice shelf. The route becomes less steep, but crevasses and short sections of icefall must be crossed. There is still substantial exposure to objective hazards as the route continues along this slanting shelf to the top of Gibraltar Rock (Camp Comfort) or the upper Nisqually Glacier. This section of the route changes from year to year. Glacier movement pushes the old shelf onto the Nisqually Glacier and usually creates another one behind it.

To ascend the **Nisqually Cleaver route**, climb the steep face and snow

Climbers above 12,000 feet on Nisqually Cleaver, with the Nisqually Glacier falls below © George Beilstein

chutes, keeping the rock bands on the left and the Nisqually Ice Cliff and shelf to the right. Variations exist that may include short water-ice steps to 80 degrees. The rock bands at 12,500 feet can either be climbed (moves are easy but exposure is great) or circumnavigated as seasonal conditions dictate. The route is quite airy through this section. After the rock bands, traverse and climb left around the nose or crest of the upper cleaver to the upper Nisqually Icefall. Stay close to the cleaver and climb another chute, angled at 40 degrees, to the termination of the cleaver.

After this climb of either the Nisqually Ice Cliff or Cleaver, ascend glacier slopes to the summit crater rim. It's a 20-minute walk to Columbia Crest from the crater rim.

Descent: Descend the Ingraham Direct, Disappointment Cleaver, or Gibraltar Ledges back to high camp.

Nisqually Icefall

The Nisqually Icefall, like the Nisqually Ice Cliff and Cleaver, is a great winter and spring climb. Ascending the largest glacier on the south side of the mountain, this route avoids many of the hazards that make Gibraltar Chute, Nisqually Ice Cliff, and Nisqually Cleaver so dangerous. However, there still are objec-

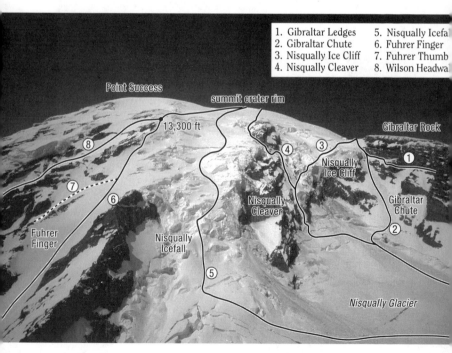

1. Gibraltar Ledges
2. Gibraltar Chute
3. Nisqually Ice Cliff
4. Nisqually Cleaver
5. Nisqually Icefall
6. Fuhrer Finger
7. Fuhrer Thumb
8. Wilson Headwall

tive hazards and they can be substantial depending on the year. The icefall's charms include excellent views of the Nisqually Basin and river drainage and the Paradise area, and a close-up look at such glacier features as seracs, jumbled ice blocks, and crevasses. Climbers need good routefinding and glacier navigation skills; a speedy ascent is strongly recommended. Avoid the icefall late in the summer, when the glacier becomes extremely broken and navigation too circuitous.

For additional general information related to this route, see the introduction to the Gibraltar Chute route.

ELEVATION GAIN: 9,000 feet from Paradise to Columbia Crest.

WHAT TO EXPECT: Substantial exposure to icefall; 35- to 60-degree snow and ice slopes. Grade II or III.

TIME: 2 to 3 days; 7 to 10 hours from high camp to summit, 3 to 5 hours for descent to high camp.

SEASON: Winter through June.

FIRST ASCENT: Dee Molenaar and Robert Craig; July 15, 1948.

HIGH CAMP: At the base of the Cowlitz Cleaver, just below Camp Muir, on the edge of the Nisqually Glacier (9,800 feet); or at Camp Muir (10,080 feet).

From the base of Cowlitz Cleaver (9,800 feet), climb and traverse west onto the Nisqually toward the lower and western lobe of the glacier. There is some danger of rockfall and icefall from the upper Nisqually, so move quickly. Begin climbing the icefall at 10,800 feet, negotiating crevasses, seracs, and other features.

The glacier is not very steep, but there may be short sections of vertical ice where belays and protection are needed to navigate around obstructions. Beware of hidden crevasses; winter snowfall deceptively hides a very active and broken icefall.

Ascend to 12,500 feet, where steepness of the icefall decreases. The Nisqually Cleaver is on your right, and the top of upper Wapowety Cleaver will be on your left; ascend gentle glacier slopes to the crater rim. It's a 20-minute walk to Columbia Crest from the crater rim.

Descent: Descend the Ingraham Direct, Disappointment Cleaver, or Gibraltar Ledges back to high camp.

WAPOWETY CLEAVER AND KAUTZ ROUTES

The Wapowety Cleaver and Kautz routes on the south side encompass some of Mount Rainier's most noted climbs. These are moderately popular climbs for mountaineers seeking ascents on nonstandard routes. The high camps are primitive. The routes see little guided activity and are considered good alternatives to the most crowded tracks: the Ingraham Direct, Disappointment Cleaver, and Emmons Glacier. They are all Grade II or III, yet each has its own unique character.

The upper Wapowety Cleaver is a large triangular rock formation with steep snowfields and numerous snow chutes that melt out late in the summer. It separates the upper Kautz Glacier on its left (west) and the Nisqually Glacier on its right, and the bottom perimeter marks the beginning of the Wilson Glacier. From the Wilson Glacier, climbers have access to three climbing routes: the **Fuhrer Finger**, the **Fuhrer Thumb**, and the **Wilson Headwall**.

The **Kautz Glacier** flows from the summit along the western edge of the Wilson Headwall. The glacier has a prominent lobe and ice cliff that can be seen from Paradise. The **Kautz Headwall** and **Kautz Cleaver** routes ascend the volcanic rocky spur that originates at Point Success. The Kautz Cleaver is a ridge that divides the Success Glacier and its headwall from the lower Kautz Glacier. The cleaver also forms the headwall for Kautz Basin, where the upper Kautz Glacier empties from a massive ice cliff.

Getting to the high camps: Of the two principal approaches to these routes, most climbers prefer the one that begins at Paradise. The alternative approach begins much lower—at the Comet Falls trailhead (3,600 feet), 4 miles above Longmire. Starting in the forest, this approach follows the trail along Van Trump Creek, passing Comet Falls and continuing up to Van Trump Park (5,600 feet). It ascends subalpine and alpine meadows north-northeast along the lower Wapowety Cleaver, which separates the lower Kautz and Wilson Glaciers. A very beautiful hike, this approach requires substantially more elevation gain, and many climbers prefer not to walk the extra distance.

The usual approach begins at the Paradise upper parking lot (5,420 feet) and follows the Skyline Trail for 1 mile to Glacier Vista (6,336 feet), a popular day-hike destination with excellent views of Mount Rainier, Mount Adams, Mount St. Helens, and Mount Hood. The vista overlooks the Nisqually Glacier, where climbers descend 400 feet to cross the lateral moraine and get onto the glacier.

Rope up—the Nisqually has numerous hidden holes—and continue northwest across the glacier. Look for a prominent snow chute on the other side of the glacier that provides access to the west side (left side) of the Wilson Glacier and to the upper Wapowety Cleaver. A large rock buttress marks the right side of this chute, known as the Fan. There may be a bergschrund at the entrance to the chute and a creek is usually flowing from the buttress.

Wapowety and Kautz Routes
1. Fuhrer Finger
2. Fuhrer Thumb
3. Wilson Headwall
4. Kautz Glacier
5. Kautz Headwall
6. Kautz Cleaver

Point Success

13,300 ft

Kautz Glacier

Kautz Ice Cliff

Camp Hazard
11,300 ft

Wilson Headwall

safer bivy

10,200 ft

Kautz Glacier

9,200 ft

Kautz Cleaver

10,200 ft

Success Cleaver

Success Glacier

9,200 ft

To Paradise

Put your helmet on; the chute is notorious for rockfall and avalanches, and usually has a large cornice directly above. Ascend the 25- to 35-degree slope for an elevation gain of 800 feet, to where the grade relaxes and provides a good rest area with views of the Nisqually Glacier, Paradise, and Muir Snowfield.

Continue north and uphill; the grade increases to 40 degrees as it climbs around another rock buttress, this one on your left, to reach the crest of Wapowety Cleaver. Travel along the broad, snowy crest of the cleaver, heading north toward the mountain. The Wilson Headwall and Kautz Glacier are straight ahead, and the route you intend to climb will determine where you make high camp.

To reach high camps for the Fuhrer Finger, Fuhrer Thumb, Wilson Headwall, and Kautz Glacier routes, continue up the mountain, selecting a site within the permitted zone that best suits the needs of your climb. Excellent bivies exist along the cleaver, where occasional rock outcroppings provide great weather protection. Camp Hazard (11,300 feet) is the highest camp along the cleaver. The camp has established rock walls and collection barrels for blue bags, and the unique location provides great views of the southern Cascades and the Kautz Ice Cliff. Unfortunately the camp is exposed to significant rockfall and icefall from that same ice cliff. Consider a safer camp at a lower elevation, where you won't have to carry your high-camp gear so far.

To reach high camps for the Kautz Headwall and Kautz Cleaver routes, traverse westerly across the broad Wapowety Cleaver to the edge of the lower Kautz Glacier.

Fuhrer Finger and Fuhrer Thumb

The Fuhrer Finger is a wide, steep couloir up the eastern face of the Wilson Headwall. The enormity of the headwall dwarfs climbers, with large volcanic spires standing out sharply as teams cross the upper Wilson Glacier to access the Finger. The Fuhrer Finger route is recessed into the headwall, providing nonglaciated access up the wall and onto the upper western edge of the Nisqually Glacier. The route is often said to be the fastest way up the mountain, but it's not, because you spend too much time dropping down to the Nisqually Glacier and crossing it. The Gibraltar Chute offers faster access from parking lot to summit. The Fuhrer Thumb is a narrow couloir immediately west of the Finger.

This flank of Rainier receives a lot of sun. The snow may be firm early in the morning, but the routes can be an oven on clear, sunny days when the snow becomes deep and sloppy. Warmth also means rockfall; the routes demand helmets and call for a true alpine start. The routes eventually lead to

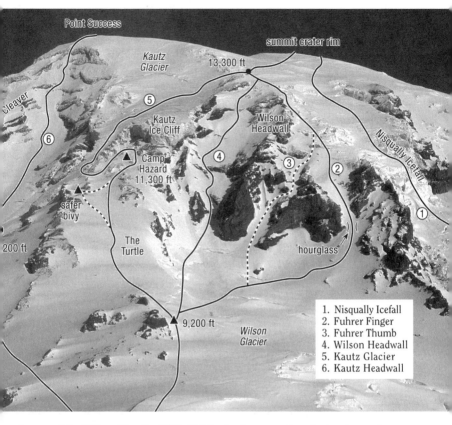

1. Nisqually Icefall
2. Fuhrer Finger
3. Fuhrer Thumb
4. Wilson Headwall
5. Kautz Glacier
6. Kautz Headwall

the top of the Wilson Headwall (13,300 feet), where gentler glacier slopes then take climbers to the summit crater rim and Columbia Crest.

ELEVATION GAIN: 9,000 feet from Paradise to Columbia Crest.

WHAT TO EXPECT: Rockfall hazard; avalanche danger; glacier travel; 30- to 45-degree snow and ice slopes. Grade II.

TIME: 2 to 4 days; 5 to 7 hours from high camp to summit, 3 to 5 hours for descent to high camp.

SEASON: December through early August.

FIRST ASCENT: Fuhrer Finger—Hans Fuhrer, Heinie Fuhrer, Joseph Hazard, Peyton Farrer, and Thomas Hermans; July 2, 1920. Fuhrer Thumb—Jim Wickwire, Charlie Raymond, and Tom Stewart; May 27, 1972.

HIGH CAMP: On the west edge of Wilson Glacier, at 9,200 feet, next to a large rock buttress that provides excellent weather protection.

From the 9,200-foot high camp, traverse north-northeast across Wilson Glacier toward the eastern flank of the Wilson Headwall. Take care along the Wilson

Glacier because many crevasses run parallel to the route, and arresting a crevasse fall is problematic.

The **Fuhrer Finger route** is a prominent snow couloir with an hourglass funnel. Ascend the glacier to the base of the Finger at 10,000 feet, where there may be a bergschrund late in the season. Begin the 2,000-foot climb up the couloir. The route looks steep from a distance; however, the slope angle is between 30 and 45 degrees. Move quickly, as rockfall is prevalent in the hourglass, a feature more prominent in the summer. The Finger broadens above 11,300 feet.

The **Fuhrer Thumb route** ascends one of the snow couloirs immediately west of the Fuhrer Finger. From the 9,200-foot high camp, approach the Fuhrer Finger, but head west and instead climb the prominent narrow couloir between the Wilson Headwall and the Finger. The Thumb has similar slope angles and hazards as the Finger, but it is considerably narrower. This couloir reconnects with Fuhrer Finger around 11,500 feet. (Avoid the temptation to continue up

snow couloirs that ascend the headwall more directly; they end in cliffs.)

From 11,500 feet, Fuhrer Finger continues until it tops out onto the eastern edge of the Wilson Headwall, next to the Nisqually Glacier, at about 12,000 feet. Climb along the edge of the glacier to the crest of the headwall at 13,300 feet. From here, it's a short climb to the summit crater rim and Columbia Crest.

Descent: There are several choices. Teams can descend the Fuhrer Finger, the Kautz Glacier route, or a standard route back to Camp Muir.

Teams that descend the Finger are often tempted to glissade, but don't. This route has slid on many parties, and is the perfect angle for such an incident. Move quickly, and beware of avalanches in spring and early summer.

The recommended descent is via the Kautz Glacier. This descent provides a loop trip back to high camp on the west edge of Wilson Glacier, and doesn't require climbers to traverse back across the upper Wilson Glacier.

A descent via the Ingraham Glacier Direct, Disappointment Cleaver, or Gibraltar Ledges to Camp Muir and down to Paradise is popular with teams that want to sleep on the summit, carry over, or avoid the climb back out of the lower Nisqually Glacier up to Glacier Vista.

Wilson Glacier Headwall

The Wilson Glacier Headwall is a steep cirque of snowfields and rock bands accessed through narrow couloirs off the northwest head of the Wilson Glacier. The headwall comprises the central and western side of Wapowety Cleaver and tops out at 13,300 feet, the cleaver's apex. The climb is best attempted when snow covers most of the face. There is substantial exposure to icefall from the Kautz Ice Cliff when accessing the headwall. Climbers should use helmets and get an alpine start, especially in summer, when the headwall gets a lot of sun. Once on the route, the climb is moderately steep with great exposure as the lower headwall and Wilson Glacier fall away below.

ELEVATION GAIN: 9,000 feet from Paradise to Columbia Crest.

WHAT TO EXPECT: Rockfall and icefall hazards; glacier travel; 30- to 50-degree snow and ice slopes. Grade II or III.

TIME: 2 to 4 days; 6 to 9 hours from high camp to summit, 3 to 5 hours for descent to high camp.

SEASON: Winter through July.

FIRST ASCENT: Dee Molenaar and Pete Schoening; July 21, 1957.

HIGH CAMP: On the west edge of Wilson Glacier, at 9,200 feet, next to a large rock buttress that provides excellent weather protection.

From the 9,200-foot high camp, climb directly to the headwall and across the top of the Wilson Glacier. There may be a bergschrund in late season.

summit crater rim

Upper
Nisqually
Glacier

Nisqually
Glacier

Nisqually
Icefall

13,300 ft

Wilson
Headwall

Kautz
Glacier

Point Success

Camp
Hazard
11,300 ft

safer
bivy

The
Turtle

9,200 ft

10,200 ft

Wilson
Glacier

1. Nisqually Ice Cliff
2. Nisqually Cleaver
3. Nisqually Icefall
4. Fuhrer Finger
5. Fuhrer Thumb
6. Wilson Headwall
7. Kautz Glacier
8. Kautz Headwall
9. Kautz Cleaver

Climbers made the first winter ascent of the Wilson Headwall in the winter, 1975–1976. The Kautz Ice Cliff looms in the background. © *Eric Simonson*

The headwall is accessed through 30-degree snow chutes (at 10,000 feet) that expose climbers to icefall from the Kautz Ice Cliff. Move quickly.

Stay left of the prominent rock buttress in the center of the headwall and ascend 30- to 45-degree slopes for 3,000 feet. The steepest sections are lower on the face, increasing the feeling of exposure higher on the route. Small rock bands at 11,300 feet and 12,200 feet can be climbed or bypassed on the sides.

Slope angle decreases higher on the snowfield, but larger bands of rock near the top of the upper Wapowety Cleaver may require fifth-class moves and protection. These can be avoided by exiting on the eastern snow chute toward the upper Nisqually Glacier. Either way, continue to 13,300 feet—the top of the headwall and of Wapowety Cleaver. From here, it's a short climb to the summit crater rim and Columbia Crest.

Descent: Teams usually descend the Kautz Glacier route, which provides a loop trip back to the high camp, or carry over the summit and take a standard route back to Camp Muir. It's best to avoid descending the headwall because the hazards loom larger later in the day, and the steepness of the route makes descent difficult.

A descent via the Ingraham Glacier Direct, Disappointment Cleaver, or Gibraltar Ledges to Camp Muir and down to Paradise is popular with teams wishing to camp on the summit, carry over, or avoid the climb back out of the lower Nisqually Glacier up to Glacier Vista.

Kautz Glacier

The Kautz Glacier is the original line taken by Lieutenant Kautz and his party when they nearly reached the summit in July 1857. A long approach combined with glacier travel and steep pitches of frozen snow or ice make this route an attractive choice for mountaineers desiring a challenging intermediate climb of Mount Rainier.

The Kautz Ice Cliff looms above climbers as they approach the route. Camp Hazard (11,300 feet) has the distinction of being the highest established camp on the mountain. The camp has protective rock walls piled up by climbers long ago, and collection barrels for blue bags. Despite the amenities, climbers should avoid staying here. The camp lies directly below the massive Kautz Ice Cliff, which occasionally dumps truck-size blocks of ice and debris into the camp, and sometimes even down the Turtle, the snowfield below. There are good protected bivy sites on the western edge of the Turtle.

Above Camp Hazard, climbers on the Kautz Glacier route get up-close and

Point Success

Columbia Crest

crater rim

⑤

Kautz
Glacier

④

13,300 ft

Nisqually
Glacier

Kautz
Ice Cliff

Wilson
Headwall

③

①

Camp
Hazard
11,300 ft

safer
bivy

②

'utz
cier

The
Turtle

10,200 ft

9,200 ft

Wilson
Glacier

. Fuhrer Finger
. Fuhrer Thumb
. Wilson Headwall
. Kautz Glacier
. Kautz Headwall
. Kautz Cleaver

personal with the ice cliff, its seracs, and blue ice pinnacles. From 1939 to 1950, the Kautz Glacier was the standard route for guided parties.

ELEVATION GAIN: 9,000 feet from Paradise to Columbia Crest.

WHAT TO EXPECT: Rockfall and icefall hazards; glacier travel; 50- to 60-degree snow and ice slopes. Grade II or III.

TIME: 2 to 4 days; 5 to 10 hours from high camp to summit (depending on the high camp), 3 to 5 hours for descent to high camp.

SEASON: A great climb year-round; late-season ascents demand good technical ice skills to move through dangerous areas quickly.

FIRST ASCENT: Three women and seven men were reported to have climbed the route in 1913. The first recorded ascent was by Hans Fuhrer, Heinie Fuhrer, Roger Toll, and Harry Myers; July 28, 1920.

HIGH CAMP: Bivouac platforms can be dug in the snow along the western edge of the Turtle, a broad, rolling snow slope below Camp Hazard, between 9,800 and 11,000 feet.

From high camp, climb to the base of the Kautz Ice Cliff (11,300 feet). Head left (west) and descend 200 feet down an ice gully walled off on the right by the ice cliff and on the left by steep, rocky cliffs. Move quickly and wear a helmet; this is a run-out for ice-cliff debris.

Continue along the base of the ice cliff and skirt its bottom. Then ascend

steep snow and ice slopes that provide access to the glacier above the ice cliff. There are two pitches of 50- to 60-degree frozen snow or hard glacial ice, separated by about 100 yards of gentler glacier. The second pitch is a bit longer and steeper than the first; ice screws or pickets are recommended for protection.

The angle relaxes at the top of the second steep pitch, and glacier travel resumes to the apex of Wapowety Cleaver (13,300 feet). Continue along the upper Kautz and Nisqually Glaciers to the south side of the summit crater rim. From there, the true summit at Columbia Crest is a 15-minute walk away.

Descent: Climbers usually descend the Kautz Glacier, though some choose a summit carry-over and a standard route back to Camp Muir. When descending the Kautz Glacier, use extra caution on the steep icy pitches. Climbers with limited experience should descend on belay or consider rappelling. Ice pinnacles or constructed bollards make possible rappel anchors.

Descending the Ingraham Glacier Direct, Disappointment Cleaver, or Gibraltar Ledges to Camp Muir is popular with teams wishing to camp on the summit, carry over, or avoid the climb back out of the lower Nisqually Glacier up to Glacier Vista.

Kautz Headwall

The Kautz Headwall, which is rarely climbed, is one of the longest headwalls on Mount Rainier. A lengthy approach and ominous appearance discourage many climbers from attempting the route. High camp on Wapowety Cleaver sits above the lower Kautz Glacier. From there, climbers have an excellent view of the route, which crosses under the lower lobe of the Kautz Ice Cliff and ascends the right side of Kautz Cleaver to Point Success.

The headwall has moderately steep snowfields, rock bands, and occasional short sections of water ice in June and July. The route ascends technical climbing terrain for over 3,500 feet, making for some exciting climbing with great exposure. As with other headwalls, the climb has late-season rockfall problems.

ELEVATION GAIN: 9,000 feet from Paradise to Columbia Crest.

WHAT TO EXPECT: Rockfall and icefall hazards; glacier travel; 50-degree snow and ice slopes with rock bands. Grade III.

TIME: 2 to 4 days; 6 to 9 hours from high camp to summit, 3 to 6 hours for descent to high camp.

SEASON: December through July.

FIRST ASCENT: Pat Callis, Dan Davis, and Don Gordon; July 8, 1963.

HIGH CAMP: Bivouac platforms can be dug in the snow between 9,500 and 10,200 feet on the edge of Wapowety Cleaver.

Access the lower Kautz Glacier by dropping off Wapowety Cleaver and descending scree and snow slopes. The Kautz Headwall lies directly north; however,

Point Success

13,300 ft

Kautz
Ice Cliff

Camp
Hazard

11,300 ft

10,200 ft

Kautz
Glacier

Kautz
Glacier

10,200 ft

Tahoma
Cleaver

Success
Cleaver

1. Kautz Glacier
2. Kautz Headwall
3. Kautz Cleaver
4. Success Cleaver

climbers must first cross under the lower lobe of the Kautz Ice Cliff. Debris on the glacier will indicate recent activity. Move quickly through this area of high objective hazard. Continue climbing toward the headwall, looking for a good location to cross the bergschrund and access the face.

The grade starts at 30 degrees, but sections of the climb may reach 50 or 60 degrees depending on the season. Summer ascent teams may even find short sections (10 to 20 feet) of water ice over some of the rock bands. Continue to ascend chutes and snowfields left toward the crest of Kautz Cleaver. The final rock bands can either be climbed directly or skirted to the left, where a short terraced ledge leads to Point Success. Bring pickets for protection. From Point Success, cross the narrow col and ascend gentle slopes for the half-hour walk to Columbia Crest.

Descent: Descend the Kautz Glacier route. Take caution on the steep icy pitches, where climbers may elect to downclimb on belay or possibly rappel.

Kautz Cleaver

The Kautz Cleaver is a long rocky ridge that separates the Success and Kautz Glaciers. Beginning at 8,800 feet, the cleaver rises over 5,000 feet through snow ramps, rock bands, and scree slopes to Point Success. This route is best climbed when there is plenty of snow covering the loose rock and pumice that makes up most of this ridge. Although the route is technically easy, it sees little climbing activity due to its long approach.

The quickest approach may be via the Comet Falls trailhead, 4 miles up the road from Longmire, instead of from Paradise; it's a toss up. The Comet Falls approach begins much lower—at 3,600 feet, instead of the Paradise elevation of 5,420—but it's more direct, sending climbers straight up Wapowety Cleaver. The Kautz Cleaver is a great moderate climb for teams looking to get off the beaten track, away from crowded high camps and routes.

ELEVATION GAIN: 9,000 feet from Paradise to Columbia Point (or 11,200 feet from the Comet Falls trailhead to Columbia Crest).

WHAT TO EXPECT: Rockfall hazard; glacier travel; 30-degree snow slopes with rock bands. Grade II.

TIME: 2 to 4 days; 7 to 10 hours to high camp, 7 to 10 hours from high camp to summit, 3 to 6 hours for descent to high camp.

SEASON: Winter through July.

FIRST ASCENT: George Senner and Charles Robinson; September 1, 1957.

HIGH CAMP: On the Kautz Cleaver (at 10,200 feet) or on Wapowety Cleaver (at 9,000 feet).

From 8,000 feet on Wapowety Cleaver, descend to the lower Kautz Glacier and navigate through crevasse fields to the toe of Kautz Cleaver at 8,800 feet. Gain

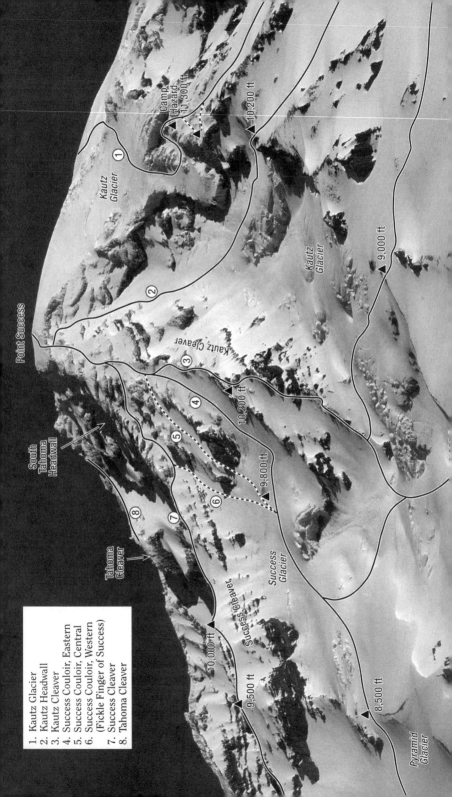

Point Success

Camp
Hazard
(11,300 ft)

10,200 ft

Kautz
Glacier

Kautz
Glacier

9,000 ft

①

②

Kautz Cleaver

③

④

10,200 ft

⑤

9,800 ft

South
Tahoma
Headwall

⑥

⑦

⑧

Tahoma
Cleaver

Success Cleaver

Success
Glacier

10,000 ft

9,500 ft

8,500 ft

Pyramid
Glacier

1. Kautz Glacier
2. Kautz Headwall
3. Kautz Cleaver
4. Success Couloir, Eastern
5. Success Couloir, Central
6. Success Couloir, Western
   (Fickle Finger of Success)
7. Success Cleaver
8. Tahoma Cleaver

the west side of the cleaver at 9,000 feet and ascend 20- to 35-degree slopes on the left (west) of the crest to the good bivy site on the cleaver at 10,200 feet.

An alternative is to make high camp at 9,000 feet on Wapowety Cleaver. From camp, descend onto the lower Kautz Glacier and traverse across crevasse fields to Kautz Cleaver. Gain the eastern side of the cleaver on 30-degree snow slopes at about 9,500 feet. Ascend directly to the ridge crest and saddle at 10,200 feet.

From 10,200 feet, the climb offers a variety of options. Ascend the ridge via any number of chutes and gullies, generally staying on the western flank. At 12,000 feet, the cleaver broadens and the Success Cleaver route joins in. From here, stay east of the cleaver's crest, climbing high above the Kautz Headwall. The slope angle increases to 40 degrees for a short pitch before topping out at Point Success. From Point Success, cross the narrow col and ascend gentle slopes for the half-hour walk to Columbia Crest.

Descent: Descend the climbing route.

LONGMIRE AND WESTSIDE ROAD APPROACHES

There are nine major climbing routes and several variations on Mount Rainier's southwest aspect. All can be accessed from the Westside Road and Longmire area.

These climbs are categorized by proximity to prominent mountain features: Success Cleaver, Tahoma Cleaver, or Puyallup Cleaver.

Success Cleaver routes	**Puyallup Cleaver routes**
Success Couloirs	Tahoma Glacier
Success Cleaver	Tahoma Sickle
South Tahoma Headwall	Sunset Amphitheater Icecap
	Sunset Amphitheater Headwall Couloir
Tahoma Cleaver route	Sunset Ridge
Tahoma Cleaver	

The routes in this section represent some of the longest and most challenging on Mount Rainier. They see limited use, though most are climbed annually and are popular with climbers familiar with Cascades volcano mountaineering. The long approaches, technical difficulties, and sporadic climbing activity make these routes committing. Climbing them requires self-reliance, as rangers and other mountaineers are few and far between. These cautions add to the attraction of solitude and wilderness experience, and the Park Service has tighter backcountry camping limitations to preserve the integrity of the area.

Many of these routes top out on either Point Success (14,158 feet) or Liberty Cap (14,112 feet). Both destinations require an additional hike to the true 14,410-foot summit at Columbia Crest. From Point Success, it's a half-hour walk to Columbia Crest. From Liberty Cap, it's a walk of nearly a mile to Columbia Crest, and climbers must descend to the col at 13,600 feet before regaining the gentle slopes to 14,410 feet.

Longmire is a popular stopping point for visitors on the way to Paradise. Longmire has a Park Service museum, wilderness information center, and hotel with restaurant and gift shop. Obtain climbing and backcountry permits for these routes at the wilderness information center during the summer and at the museum in the fall, winter, and spring. There are no services along the Westside Road, where many of these routes are best approached.

The unpaved Westside Road leaves from the main park road at a point

1. Success Couloir, Eastern
2. Success Couloir, Central and
   Western
3. Success Cleaver
4. South Tahoma Headwall,
   Success Cleaver approach
5. South Tahoma Headwall
6. Tahoma Cleaver, lower buttress
7. Tahoma Cleaver

8. Tahoma Glacier, Tahoma
   Cleaver approach
9. Tahoma Glacier
10. Tahoma Glacier, the Sickle
11. Tahoma Glacier, early season
    approach
12. Sunset Amphitheater Ice Cap
    and Headwall Couloir
13. Sunset Ridge

Success Cleaver

Point Success

South
Tahoma
Headwall

Tahoma
Cleaver

Liberty Cap

Sunset Amphitheater

Sunset Ridge

Puyallup Cleaver

South Tahoma Glacier

Tahoma Glacier

Glacier Island

▼ 9,800 ft

10,000 ft

10,500 ft

▼ 11,300 ft

9,200 ft

1 mile east of the Nisqually Entrance (and 5 miles west of Longmire). The Westside Road is closed at Fish Creek, 3 miles from the turnoff, at a small parking lot. The Westside Road gave vehicle access to the interior of the park's west side and the Wonderland Trail until severe flooding from Tahoma Creek in the 1986 washed out the road. Attempts to repair it have met with opposition from the creek. The Park Service has been considering a van shuttle service to carry visitors up the road beyond the washout, unless an affordable way can be found to permanently repair the road.

SUCCESS CLEAVER ROUTES

The Success Cleaver routes—Success Couloirs, Success Cleaver, and South Tahoma Headwall—have the distinction of being some of the longest on Mount Rainier. Starting at 2,880 feet on the Westside Road or at 2,760 feet at Longmire, climbers ascend through old-growth forest to the alpine meadows of Indian Henrys Hunting Ground and Pyramid Peak.

Some teams elect to spend 2 days approaching these climbs. This eases the work of ascending more than 11,000 feet to the summit. These routes see little activity; expect postholing through soft snow that impedes even the strongest teams. All three of these routes should be climbed when there is plenty of snow covering the rotten rock and pumice that make up the terrain.

Getting to the high camps: These routes have different high camps and three possible approaches. All approaches share an incredible hike through old-growth forest to the sub-alpine meadows of Indian Henrys Hunting Ground. There, they join together at the Mirror Lake Trail and continue towards the mountain.

For the approach from Longmire (2,760 feet), take the Rampart Ridge Trail for 1.4 miles to the Wonderland Trail. Take the Wonderland Trail north to Indian Henrys Hunting Ground, passing Devil's Dream Camp (5 miles from Longmire) and the ranger patrol cabin at Indian Henrys (6 miles from Longmire). Continue north on the Wonderland Trail for three-tenths of a mile past the patrol cabin and turn right (north) on the Mirror Lake Trail.

From Kautz Creek trailhead and picnic area 3.5 miles inside the Nisqually Entrance, take the Kautz Creek Trail north 5.7 miles to Indian Henrys Hunting Ground and ranger patrol cabin. There, the trail intersects with the Wonderland Trail. Turn left and continue north on the Wonderland Trail three-tenths mile to the Mirror Lake trail, where this time you'll turn right (north), and follow the trial.

To reach this Mirror Lake Trail junction via the approach from the

Westside Road, begin on the road at its closure at Fish Creek (2,880 feet). Hike for 1 mile along the closed road, paralleling Tahoma Creek through the washout to the first sharp left-hand bend in the road. From this sharp turn, look for a newly established section of trail on the right-hand side rather than continuing uphill on the road toward Round Pass. (This section of the old Tahoma Creek Trail was washed out with the road.) Get on the new section, which soon rejoins the old Tahoma Creek Trail, hiking for 2.2 miles from the Westside Road to the trail's T intersection with the Wonderland Trail near the Tahoma Creek suspension bridge. (The old Tahoma Creek Trail is no longer indicated on many maps, even though it is still accessible and in good traveling shape.) Turn right on the Wonderland Trail, cross the suspension bridge, and continue toward Indian Henrys Hunting Ground. Look for the intersection with the Mirror Lake Trail at 1.2 miles from the bridge, and turn north (left) onto that trail.

All approaches bring you to the Mirror Lake Trail, which ascends through subalpine meadows to the base of Pyramid Peak. The terrain becomes alpine as you skirt the northwest shoulder of Pyramid Peak (at an elevation of 5,600 feet) and continue up the broad slopes of lower Success Cleaver. Pyramid Peak makes a great side trip with excellent views, but don't attempt to downclimb the north side back to lower Success Cleaver; it's steep, with loose rocks.

Climb Success Cleaver to between 7,500 and 8,500 feet. Climbers planning to ascend the Success Couloirs route should then head northeast onto the Pyramid and Success Glaciers. If you intend to climb the Success Cleaver route, continue up the cleaver. For the South Tahoma Headwall route, head north onto the South Tahoma Glacier.

Success Couloirs
Eastern, Central, and Western (Fickle Finger of Success)

These moderately steep snow couloirs rise from Success Glacier to the upper Kautz and Success Cleavers. There are three major couloirs—the eastern of which saw the first ascent—all of similar grade and challenge. These routes see little climbing activity. The couloirs are most enjoyably climbed when there is sufficient snow to cover the loose rock and pumice that constitute the underlying terrain.

Snowboarders and skiers have descended the climbing lines, some from Point Success. The headwall's southern aspect makes great corn snow on warm, sunny days, and the lack of crevasse difficulties makes the ride easier

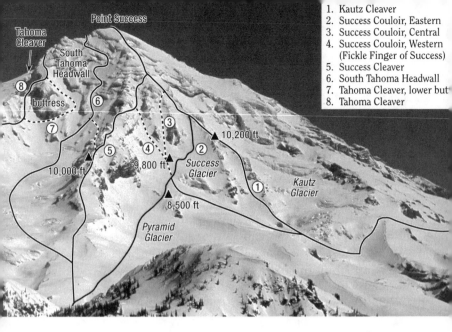

1. Kautz Cleaver
2. Success Couloir, Eastern
3. Success Couloir, Central
4. Success Couloir, Western (Fickle Finger of Success)
5. Success Cleaver
6. South Tahoma Headwall
7. Tahoma Cleaver, lower but
8. Tahoma Cleaver

to navigate. The routes are steep, up to 45 degrees or more, and are prime avalanche terrain, so the descent is for accomplished snowboarders and skiers only.

ELEVATION GAIN: About 11,400 feet from either Longmire or the Westside Road to Point Success.

WHAT TO EXPECT: Glacier travel; 30- to 50-degree slopes. Grade II.

TIME: 2 to 4 days; 8 to 10 hours from high camp to summit, 3 to 4 hours for descent to high camp.

SEASON: April through July.

FIRST ASCENT: Eastern Couloir—George Senner and Dick Walstrom; July 17, 1960. Central Couloir—James Couch party; 1987. Fickle Finger of Success—Alex Van Steen, Richard Alpert, David Branton, Mark Kelly, Steve Northern, and Pete Laird; July 25, 1997.

HIGH CAMP: From the approach at 7,500 to 8,000 feet on lower Success Cleaver, cross north on Pyramid Glacier. Camp on the small ridge separating the Pyramid and Success Glaciers, 8,500 feet, or continue farther and bivy on the Success Glacier itself, 9,800 feet. Do not camp too close to the couloirs, because avalanches from the headwall can bury camps.

Ascend north on the Success Glacier toward the base of the headwall. For the eastern couloir, cross the bergschrund near 10,000 feet and ascend the 30- to 40-degree snow slopes to the upper Kautz Cleaver, a rather straight-forward climb. For the central couloir, cross the bergschrund near 10,400 feet and ascend similar grade slopes to the apex of the couloir. Depending on the yearly snowfall, there may be a short rock band to negotiate. Climb right (east) near the apex and ascend through the narrow rock band to gain the upper eastern couloir and Kautz Cleaver near 12,000 feet.

For the western couloir, or Fickle Finger of Success, ascend the Success Glacier to 10,000 feet and cross the bergschrund. The couloir climbs 40-degree snow slopes to gain the upper Success Cleaver route near 11,600 feet. Depending on the yearly snowfall, there may be a short rock band to cross or steep bulge in the snow slope, perhaps 50 degrees to gain upper Success Cleaver. From there, ascend and traverse similar grade snow and ice slopes on the eastern aspect of the cleaver crest to join the upper Kautz Cleaver route near 12,000 feet.

Above there, the climb becomes steep, 40- to 50-degrees, near 13,900 feet for a pitch or two. The Kautz Headwall falls 3,500 feet precipitously below, so teams may elect to use pickets. Finish on easier snow slopes to Point Success.

Descent: Descend the route back to high camp.

Success Cleaver

Touted as one of the longest climbs on Mount Rainier, Success Cleaver is one of the few routes on which climbers can ascend to the summit without setting foot on a glacier. The cleaver begins at Pyramid Peak, rising upon broad, gentle alpine slopes. The cleaver becomes steeper and narrower as it climbs more than 7,000 feet in elevation to Point Success.

Bivouac sites along the cleaver are dramatic. Slopes fall nearly a thousand feet on either side to Success and South Tahoma Glaciers. The climbing is not too difficult, though the final pitches to Point Success are steep, and exposure is great. Success Cleaver is alpine climbing drama.

ELEVATION GAIN: About 11,400 feet from either Longmire or the Westside Road to Point Success.

WHAT TO EXPECT: Rockfall hazard; 30- to 45-degree slopes. Grade II.

TIME: 2 to 4 days; 8 to 10 hours from high camp to summit, 3 to 4 hours for descent to high camp.

SEASON: April through July.

FIRST ASCENT: Ernest Dudley and John Glascock; July 24, 1905.

HIGH CAMP: Tent platforms can be dug in the snow along the cleaver's crest up to 10,500 feet. At 9,500 feet is a site with room for a few tents.

From the 7,000-foot elevation on the lower slopes of Success Cleaver beyond Pyramid Peak, ascend northeast toward the mountain over rolling, snowy terrain. Stay on the crest or immediately to the right (east) and ascend the gradually narrowing slope. The climbing isn't too steep—35 degrees—but the route crosses atop many steep chutes that fall precipitously to Success Glacier.

Above 10,500 feet, the route leaves the cleaver's crest, heading east as it traverses and climbs onto the headwall above Success Glacier. Continue climbing 30- to 40-degree slopes to the merging of the Kautz and Success Cleavers at 12,000 feet. Again the route swings onto the southeast side of the crest, along the upper Kautz Headwall, and climbs to Point Success. The final rock bands are climbed through steep snow gullies, sometimes at 45 de-

1. Kautz Cleaver
2. Success Couloir, Eastern
3. Success Couloir, Central and We
4. Success Cleaver
5. South Tahoma Headwall
6. Tahoma Cleaver, lower buttress
7. Tahoma Cleaver

grees, with incredible exposure to the Kautz Glacier 3,500 feet below.

Since the route does not require any glacier travel, rope use is recommended only for parties that intend to belay pitches or fix protection. If a roped climber fell without a belay or fixed protection, it is unlikely that other team members could self-arrest to stop the fall, and they could be pulled off also.

Descent: Descend the route back to high camp. This is a long descent. Be extra careful because there is minimal room for mistakes, and the moderately steep slopes are unforgiving in an accident.

South Tahoma Headwall

Possibly the longest of the headwall routes on Mount Rainier, the South Tahoma Headwall sees little climbing activity. On December 10, 1946, a Marine Corps transport plane crashed into the South Tahoma Glacier, killing all thirty-two people aboard. The route was closed for a few years because of the crash; rumors of its continued closure are inaccurate, and climbers are allowed

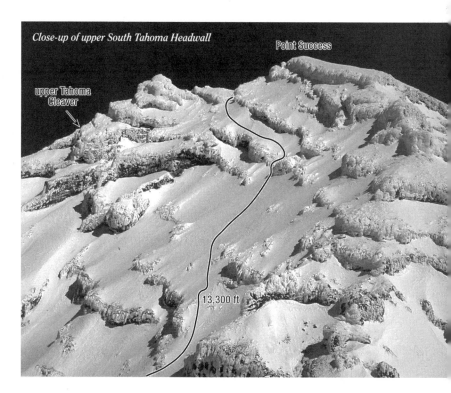

Close-up of upper South Tahoma Headwall

Point Success

upper Tahoma Cleaver

13,300 ft

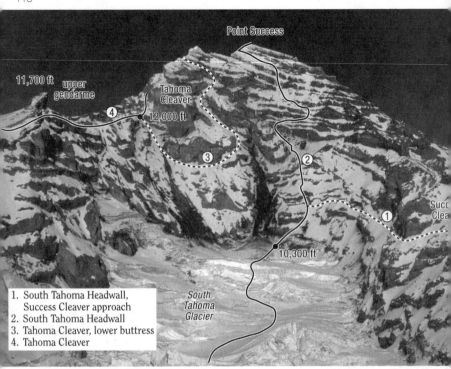

Point Success

11,700 ft upper gendarme

Tahoma Cleaver

4

12,000 ft

3

2

Succ Clea

1

10,300 ft

South Tahoma Glacier

1. South Tahoma Headwall,
   Success Cleaver approach
2. South Tahoma Headwall
3. Tahoma Cleaver, lower buttress
4. Tahoma Cleaver

to ascend the glacier and headwall. The headwall is nearly 4,000 feet high. Rising from the bergschrund at 10,300 feet on the South Tahoma Glacier, the route ascends steep snowfields and chutes as it climbs through terraced rock bands to Point Success. This climb has big air.

ELEVATION GAIN: About 11,400 feet from either Longmire or the Westside Road to Point Success.

WHAT TO EXPECT: Rockfall hazard; 30- to 55-degree slopes. Grade III.

TIME: 2 to 4 days; 8 to 10 hours from high camp to summit, 3 to 4 hours for descent to high camp.

SEASON: May through July.

FIRST ASCENT: Steve Marts and Fred Beckey; July 12, 1963.

HIGH CAMP: Camp between 8,000 and 8,300 feet on lower Success Cleaver or as high as 10,000 feet on the cleaver, depending on the route you take to get onto the headwall.

From the 8,300-foot elevation of Success Cleaver, ascend north across the South Tahoma Glacier toward the headwall. The glacier becomes severely broken in

July and August. Navigate crevasse fields to the bergschrund at the base of the headwall at about 10,300 feet.

The headwall route climbs the central face up 40- to 55-degree snow or ice slopes. Stay right of the large couloir that falls from the northwest side (left) of the headwall and the upper Tahoma Cleaver. This gully dumps substantial debris from the upper mountain and Tahoma Cleaver.

Conditions on the headwall may be hard and icy, with 30- to 50-foot sections of steep ice that bypass rock bands. The route navigates through terraced ledges, at times jogging right, then left, high onto the upper ledges of the headwall. There are multiple route possibilities, and climbers should determine their line depending on current conditions. Above 13,800 feet, continue left, gaining the upper Tahoma Cleaver on the second of the highest headwall ledges. Continue around the cleaver and ascend the glaciated slopes to Point Success.

Approach Variation: If the glacier is too broken for navigation, you can ascend Success Cleaver to 10,000 feet and traverse onto the headwall through an exposed ledge system. This approach avoids the glacier and is not steep or technical, but there is no room for error as the route traverses 30- to 45-degree slopes. Teams that choose to rope up should place fixed protection, because it's unlikely that climbers could use self-arrest successfully to stop the fall of a ropemate on such steep, hard terrain.

Descent: Because of the consistently steep nature of this route, it is best to avoid descending the South Tahoma Headwall. Instead, descend Success Cleaver, keeping in mind that there is minimal room for mistakes on its moderately steep slopes.

TAHOMA CLEAVER ROUTE

A single major climbing route ascends from the Tahoma Cleaver approach, and that is the cleaver itself. The route is hard, classic Cascades volcano mountaineering.

Getting to Tahoma Cleaver and high camp: From the Westside Road at Fish Creek (2,880 feet), take the Tahoma Creek Trail 2.2 miles to the Wonderland Trail. Head left (north) on the Wonderland Trail, ascending Emerald Ridge. The trail leaves the forest and opens to the east, exposing the vast moraines of the Tahoma Glacier. Near 5,200 feet elevation, descend east off the trail. Begin crossing the lateral moraines, heading east directly toward the large gully that divides Glacier Island, the peak that anchors the base of Tahoma Cleaver.

Along the way toward Glacier Island, Tahoma Creek must be forded below the terminus of Tahoma Glacier; keep away from the terminus to avoid rockfall danger. If the creek's current is too deep or fast, ascend onto the lower glacier and cross it to Glacier Island. Watch your footing, as occasional patches of slick, black ice are hidden under loose rocks. The lower glacier and the moraines are steep, angle-of-repose slopes filled with loose rocks, boulders, mud, pumice, and other debris. Consider wearing a helmet, and avoid climbing directly above other climbers.

A small creek drains the gully that splits Glacier Island and offers the last reliably running water along the route. Ascend the 30-degree snow gully to a large exposed rock at about 7,800 feet. Keep right of the rock as the slope exceeds 50 degrees and requires crossing a small crevasse near the top. The angle decreases considerably as the snow actually becomes the very tip of the South Tahoma Glacier. Continue on the glacial lobe for about 200 yards as the approach now climbs Tahoma Cleaver northeast toward the mountain.

From here, Mount Rainier rises unchallenged from a sea of glaciers. The view is stupendous: Success Cleaver and the South Tahoma Headwall loom to the east and northeast, while the Tahoma Glacier and Sunset Amphitheater fill the northern landscape. Turning around on a clear day reveals Mount St. Helens, seemingly a stone's throw away. The place is wild.

Now ascend snow hills that roll upward toward the impressive Red Gendarme (or Red Tower), a prominent composite rock feature at 10,000 feet, where tent platforms can be dug on the uphill side at 10,500 feet. The site holds two to five tents. If you want to camp higher, small bivy platforms can be dug around 11,300 feet, just below an upper gendarme (rock pillar) on the cleaver.

Tahoma Cleaver

Standing alone on Mount Rainier's southwest flank, Tahoma Cleaver provides one of the longest and hardest climbing routes on the mountain. The cleaver, or ridge, begins at 8,500 feet and climbs steeply to a large buttress at 12,000 feet. Above the 400- to 500-foot-high buttress, a precipitous ridge continues to Point Success. The Tahoma Cleaver separates the South Tahoma and Tahoma Glaciers.

This climb sees few ascents. The strenuous approach, rock climbing difficulties, and inherently high commitment level dissuade most mountaineers. The rock on the route is quite rotten. The climb, like all rock routes on

Point Success

South Tahoma Headwall

upper gendarme

buttress

④

⑦

⑥

10,500 ft ▲ ← Red Gendarme

▲ 9,500 ft

①

Success Cleaver

③

②

⑤

8,500 ft

Tahoma Glacier

South Tahoma Glacier

Glacier

Island

gully

1. Success Cleaver
2. South Tahoma Headwall
3. Tahoma Cleaver
4. Tahoma Cleaver, lower buttress
5. Tahoma Glacier,
   Tahoma Cleaver approach
6. Tahoma Glacier
7. Tahoma Glacier, the Sickle

moraine

fourth class
rock pitches

①

③

②

12,000 ft

Tahoma Cleaver
buttress

crest of cleaver

1. Tahoma Cleaver, lower buttress
2. Tahoma Cleaver, approximate original ascent
3. Tahoma Cleaver, ledge variation

Close-up of upper Tahoma Cleaver

Rainier, requires speed, competent skills, a helmet, and good cold conditions with plenty of snow.

ELEVATION GAIN: 11,400 feet from the Westside Road to Point Success.

WHAT TO EXPECT: Rockfall hazard; 30- to 45-degree slopes; fourth-class rock climbing. Grade III or IV.

TIME: 2 to 3 days; 7 to 10 hours from high camp to summit, carry over and descend the Tahoma Glacier.

SEASON: April through July.

FIRST ASCENT: Klindt Vielbig, Anthony Hovey, Don Keller, Paul Bellamy, and Herb Steiner; June 7, 1959. Ledge variation—Dan Davis, Gene Prater, Tom Stewart, and Steve Marts; June 16, 1968. Lower buttress variation—E. Dawes Eddy, late June 1996.

HIGH CAMP: Bivy platform in the snow on the cleaver at 10,500 feet (just above the giant Red Gendarme) or between 11,300 and 11,700 feet (below the upper gendarme).

From 11,700 feet, drop off the right (south) side of the crest about 200 feet below the upper gendarme. Climb and traverse the steep and exposed snow slopes, below several gendarmes, to regain the crest of the cleaver about 100 yards from the large buttress at 12,000 feet. Follow the cleaver to the base of the buttress, which blocks the crest. From the base, traverse and angle up the left (north) side of the cleaver on a steep ledge (ramp).

The first-ascent party climbed 40 feet along this ledge to where a 25-foot solid rock step was climbed to access the rounded snow slope above the buttress. That section of rock was later reported to have fallen away.

The **ledge variation** continues along this steep ledge, or ramp, below a 150- to 200-foot rock cliff. The ledge is exposed and, depending on the season, may have loose rock or ice. Continue along the ledge for half a mile until it peters out below the cliffs. Ascend two pitches of fourth-class rock—not difficult, but committing, steep, airy, and loose. The pitches give access to the upper Tahoma Cleaver.

For the **lower buttress variation,** stay on the right (south) side of the cleaver's crest above 11,700 feet. Instead of regaining the crest just below the buttress at 12,000 feet, continue to descend for 200 feet on the steep snow slope to the southern base of the buttress. Turn the corner and climb left up a broad, moderately steep snow slope, which gains the crest of Tahoma Cleaver above the rock buttress.

The crest of the upper cleaver is a steep, narrow snow ramp. Continue up, climbing the left-hand side of the crest to an easy 10-foot rock scramble that accesses the snow bowl below Point Success. The remaining few hundred feet are easily climbed to Point Success.

Descent: It is recommended that teams carry over on this route and descend the Tahoma Glacier.

PUYALLUP CLEAVER ROUTES

These routes derive their classification from their proximity to the Puyallup Cleaver, the long, rocky ridge that separates the Puyallup and Tahoma Glaciers. The Puyallup Cleaver, ending at 11,300 feet, does not actually gain the upper reaches of Mount Rainier. It does, however, provide access to the **Tahoma Glacier** route and to the route up the ice flow known as **the Sickle**, and also to the **Sunset Amphitheater** and **Sunset Ridge** routes. The cleaver has great vistas and offers good, well-protected camps.

Getting to the Puyallup Cleaver and high camps: The principal approach to high camp is from the Westside Road at Fish Creek, where flood damage has resulted in long-term closure to vehicles 3 miles from the start of the road. (Before the closure, climbers also had approach options via the St. Andrews Creek and South Puyallup River Trails. The trails provide direct access to the west side, but the trailheads are a long way up the closed road. Some teams choose to ride bicycles up the road, with their packs, to gain access to these trails.)

From the Westside Road closure at 2,880 feet, hike (or bicycle) 3.5 miles north to Round Pass. From Round Pass (bike rack available) take the South Puyallup River short-cut trail .6 miles (4.1 miles from trailhead) to the South Puyallup River trailhead. From there, head east up the South Puyallup River Trail 1.6 miles (5.7 miles from trailhead) to the South Puyallup River Camp and Wonderland Trail. Once there, cross the river and head north on the Wonderland Trail, climbing to St. Andrews Park 2.5 miles above (8.2 miles from the car). There, leave the trail near 6,000 feet and climb northeast through alpine meadows up the Puyallup Cleaver, passing Tokaloo Spire at 7,684 feet. Ascend the gentle snow and rock slopes of the cleaver. Excellent, well-protected bivy sites can be found along the way.

If approaching in the winter or early spring and snow is still covering the road, hike 1 mile along the Westside Road, paralleling Tahoma Creek through the washout to the first sharp left-hand bend in the road. From this sharp turn, look for a newly established section of trail on the right-hand side rather than continuing uphill on the road toward Round Pass. (The old Tahoma Creek trail was washed out with the road.) Hike on the new section, which soon rejoins the old Tahoma Creek trail, for 2.2 miles from the Westside Road to the trail's T intersection with the Wonderland Trail near the Tahoma Creek suspension bridge. During years when there is significant snowfall, it is possible to climb up a snow-filled Tahoma Creek from the road closure, avoiding the trail altogether

Southwest Mount Rainier
1. Tahoma Glacier
2. Sunset Amphitheater Ice Cap
3. Sunset Amphitheater Headwall Couloir
4. Sunset Ridge
5. Edmunds Headwall
6. Central Mowich Face

except to bypass the narrow ravine near the suspension bridge. (The Tahoma Creek Trail is no longer indicated on many maps, even though it is still accessible and in good traveling shape.)

From the T, head left (north) on the Wonderland Trail ascending Emerald Ridge to approximately 5,600 feet. As the trail opens into sub-alpine meadows, the Tahoma Glacier comes into view. Before turning west and descending to South Puyallup River, head north and ascend the glacier. In the early season it may be possible to climb the entire Tahoma Glacier from this point, otherwise, make a traverse and climb across to the Puyallup Cleaver. Gain it between 7,000 and 8,000 feet.

Climbers attempting Sunset Ridge should leave the cleaver at 8,500 feet and traverse north across the Puyallup and South Mowich Glaciers. Those headed to the Tahoma Glacier or Sunset Amphitheater routes can continue up the cleaver toward St. Andrews Rock. A great high camp can be dug at 9,200 feet below lower St. Andrews Rock.

Tahoma Glacier and the Sickle

Tahoma Glacier is the largest on Mount Rainier's west side. Spilling from the summit ice cap, the flow drains through the hourglass created between upper Tahoma Cleaver and Sunset Amphitheater. The grade decreases below 11,500 feet, where the glacier broadens and becomes a series of icefalls and crevasse fields.

One of Rainier's classic glacier climbs, the Tahoma can become very broken in late summer and a veritable oven on sunny days. The route is long by comparison with the other glacier routes. It provides excellent opportunities to practice the skills of glacier navigation, campcraft, and rescue. The glacier offers a standard route and one major variation.

ELEVATION GAIN: 11,500 feet from the Westside Road to Columbia Crest.

WHAT TO EXPECT: Glacier travel; 30- to 45-degree slopes. Grade II.

TIME: 2 to 4 days; 6 to 10 hours from high camp to summit, 3 to 5 hours for descent to high camp.

SEASON: April through early August.

FIRST ASCENT: Philemon Beecher Van Trump, Alfred Drewry, and Dr. Warren Riley; August 11, 1891. The Sickle—Leroy Ritchie, Larry Heggerness, Edward Drues, Bob Walton, Allan Van Buskirk, and Monte and Mark Haun; June 8, 1958.

HIGH CAMP: There is a nice camp at 9,200 feet on the Puyallup Cleaver, but other suitable sites can be chosen along much of the route.

From the 9,200-foot camp, ascend the Puyallup Cleaver's snow and rock slopes toward lower St. Andrews Rock.

1. South Tahoma Headwall
2. Tahoma Cleaver
3. Tahoma Glacier, Tahoma Cleaver approach
4. Tahoma Glacier
5. Tahoma Glacier, early season approach
6. Tahoma Glacier, the Sickle
7. Sunset Amphitheater Ice Cap
8. Sunset Amphitheater Headwall Couloir
9. Sunset Ridge

South Tahoma Headwall

buttress

Tahoma Cleaver

Red Gendarme

10,500 ft

12,000 ft

The Sickle

Tahoma Glacier

Liberty Cap

Sunset Amphitheater

upper St. Andrews Rock

lower St. Andrews Rock

9,200 ft

Puyallup Cleaver

Sunset Ridge

For the **standard Tahoma Glacier route:** Between 9,500 and 10,000 feet, descend the open slope on the south for 200 feet to access the Tahoma Glacier. If the glacier is heavily crevassed below lower St. Andrews Rock, continue along the Puyallup Cleaver. You can then descend the snow slopes to the Tahoma between upper and lower St. Andrews Rocks, near 10,900 feet.

Once on the glacier, negotiate crevasses and icefalls to the hourglass constriction between Tahoma Cleaver and Sunset Amphitheater. The hourglass—between 11,500 and 13,000 feet—is steep, sometimes 45 degrees, and it's common for teams to place pickets for protection. In general the glacier is most easily ascended on the north (left) side, though crevasses and glacier movement will dictate the route from year to year. The glacier may be tough to navigate, and good routefinding skills are necessary to complete the route.

Since the Tahoma Glacier can change dramatically throughout the year, several variations are possible. For the **Tahoma Cleaver approach,** start at 8,500 feet on Tahoma Cleaver, directly above Glacier Island, and traverse and climb north onto the Tahoma Glacier. The glacier can then be ascended, depending on icefalls and crevasses. This variation is best done early in the year.

For **the Sickle route:** From the top of the Puyallup Cleaver above upper St. Andrews Rock at 11,300 feet, head east onto the Tahoma Glacier and ascend the north (left) edge of the glacier up the ice flow known as the Sickle. This variation is sometimes said to remain in good shape throughout the summer, but this is not always the case. The Sickle, too, is subject to climatic changes and sometimes becomes quite broken.

Descent: Descend the Tahoma Glacier to high camp.

Sunset Amphitheater: The Ice Cap and Headwall Couloir

The Sunset Amphitheater and Headwall is a large open cirque and accumulation zone for the South Mowich Glacier. The 1,500-foot south- and west-facing walls provide a dramatic backdrop to sunsets, providing the amphitheater's romantic name. These routes are best climbed during the spring and early summer, because the South Mowich Glacier is heavily crevassed and has numerous icefalls that make the approach difficult. Also, the routes become extremely hazardous when the winter snow and ice holding the predominantly rotten rock together melts; it's best to climb when temperatures are cold. These routes rarely see activity, despite their reasonable level of challenge and beautiful location.

1. Ice Cap
2. Headwall Couloir

Liberty Cap

Sunset Ridge

Couloir

headwall

Sunset Amphitheater Ice Cap

bergschrund

bergschrund

2

1

Sunset Amphitheater

South Mowich Glacier

approx. 11,600 ft

ELEVATION GAIN: 11,400 feet from the Westside Road to Liberty Cap.

WHAT TO EXPECT: Rockfall hazard; glacier travel; 50-degree to vertical slopes. Grade III.

TIME: 2 to 4 days; 5 to 8 hours from high camp to summit, 4 to 10 hours for descent to high camp.

SEASON: April through June.

FIRST ASCENT: Sunset Amphitheater Ice Cap—J. Wendell Trosper and Fred Thieme; July 13, 1937. Headwall Couloir—The first ascent is unknown.

HIGH CAMP: There are excellent sites at 9,200 feet on the Puyallup Cleaver. Other possible bivouacs exist for teams wishing to camp closer to upper and lower St. Andrews Rocks.

From the 9,200-foot camp on Puyallup Cleaver, ascend snow and rock slopes toward lower St. Andrews Rock. If the South Mowich Glacier isn't too crevassed, ascend the left (north) side to upper St. Andrews Rock at 11,300 feet. If the

Close-up of Sunset Amphitheater Headwall Couloir

To Liberty Cap

Sunset Ridge

Sunset Amphitheater
Headwall

glacier is broken, which is likely, remain on the cleaver's crest. Climb both lower and upper St. Andrews Rocks to the top of the cleaver, where the upper Tahoma and South Mowich Glaciers separate. The cleaver is composed of loose, rotten rock, but is easy to climb.

For the **Sunset Amphitheater Ice Cap route**, ascend northeast into the Sunset Amphitheater cirque toward the lowest point in the amphitheater wall where the summit ice-cap glacier pours down a steep icefall. Find the best location to cross the bergschrund at 12,500 feet and ascend the 30- to 50-degree snow and ice slopes through a glacier hourglass to the upper ice cap. The icefall can be vertical at some locations and good glacier ice-climbing skills may be necessary. The climbing is not as hard as it may appear, but since the difficulties are high and remote, the route is committing. Once on the summit plateau, climb north on gentle glacier slopes to Liberty Cap.

The **Sunset Amphitheater Headwall Couloir route** is a steep line from the upper South Mowich Glacier to upper Sunset Ridge. From upper St. Andrews Rock, climb north into the amphitheater toward the large couloir above a glacier-draped rock buttress. Cross the bergschrund above the buttress and ascend 400 feet of couloir, then turn right to ascend and traverse another 400 feet. The steep ramp leads to some small rock bands before exiting to upper Sunset Ridge. The climb is steep, sometimes 50 degrees, and tops out at 13,200 feet on Sunset Ridge. Continue upward to the northeast and Liberty Cap.

Descent: Descend the Tahoma Glacier or Tahoma Sickle back to St. Andrews Rock and high camp.

Sunset Ridge

Separating the Sunset Amphitheater and Mowich Face, Sunset Ridge rises from a triangular base at 8,500 feet up the western corner of Mount Rainier. It is named in honor of the stellar sunsets it enjoys—weather permitting. Most of the climb itself is not a true ridge climb. Broad at its base, the route ascends a series of snowfields and gullies to gain the upper ridge near 12,000 feet.

The route alternates between the upper Mowich Face and upper Sunset Ridge to gain Liberty Cap Glacier and Liberty Cap. Climbers enjoy incredible views of the Sunset Amphitheater and Tahoma Glacier, which drops

Liberty Cap

Mowich Face

Sunset Amphitheater

11,300 ft

Sunset Ridge

10,200 ft

9,600 ft

9,200 ft

South Mowich Glacier

8,500 ft

Puyallup Glacier

1. South Mowich, approach variation to upper St. Andrews Rock
2. Sunset Amphitheater Ice Cap
3. Sunset Amphitheater Headwall Couloir
4. Sunset Ridge
5. Edmunds Headwall
6. Central Mowich Face

Facing page: A dramatic sunset from a narrow bivy, perched at 10,200 feet on Sunset Ridge

precipitously to the south. This is an excellent route with plenty of steep ice and exciting exposure.

ELEVATION GAIN: 11,400 feet from the Westside Road to Liberty Cap.

WHAT TO EXPECT: Rockfall hazard; glacier travel; 55-degree slopes. Grade III.

TIME: 2 to 4 days; .5 to 8 hours from high camp to summit, carry over and descend the Tahoma Glacier.

SEASON: April through July.

FIRST ASCENT: Lyman Boyer, Arnie Campbell, and Don Woods; August 27, 1938.

HIGH CAMP: Small platforms can be dug above 9,200 feet on the ridge, a larger more protected site exists at 9,200 feet on the divide between the South Mowich and Edmunds Glaciers.

From 8,500 feet on the Puyallup Cleaver, traverse north, crossing the Puyallup and South Mowich Glaciers. The South Mowich can be heavily crevassed. Skirt the lower rock buttress that forms the base of Sunset Ridge and ascend right (westerly) up the 30- to 40-degree snow gully to a small bergschrund below the rock bands at 9,600 feet.

Climbers can go left or right to bypass the large rock cliff above the bergschrund. The difficulties of either direction are similar as the slope angle increases slightly to a solid 45 degrees. There is a sensational tiny bivy ledge on the left-hand route at 10,200 feet, directly above a large gendarme. This pillar composed of volcanic rock and mud seems to defy gravity. The remains of a weather balloon can be spotted directly above the thin bivy ledge. Small bivy platforms can be dug if you elect to go right of the rock cliffs.

The route becomes steep and icy above 10,200 feet, with angles of 50 to 55 degrees, as it ascends a series of gullies and open faces to nearly 12,000 feet and tops out along the ridge. There are small sections of rock, but it is best to avoid these areas by staying on snow and ice slopes. The slope angle decreases for the next few hundred feet as the route climbs the ridge to 12,800 feet.

At this point, the ridge forces climbers out onto the upper Mowich Face. Traverse onto the face—a steep 50 to 55 degrees—and continue climbing to 13,200 feet, where the route regains the ridge. The slope angle continues to decrease as the route alternates along the ridge top and glacier to Liberty Cap. There may be crevasses above 13,600 feet on Liberty Cap Glacier.

Descent: This climb usually requires a carry-over unless teams elect to camp on the Puyallup Cleaver at 8,500 feet. Descend the Tahoma Glacier or Tahoma Sickle.

MOWICH LAKE AND CARBON RIVER APPROACHES

Six routes and several variations exist on Mount Rainier's northwest face and are most easily accessed from Mowich Lake.

These climbs are categorized by proximity to Ptarmigan Ridge or to the Mowich Face.

Mowich Face routes	Ptarmigan Ridge routes
Edmunds Headwall	Ptarmigan Ridge
Central Mowich Face	Ptarmigan Ice Cliff
North Mowich Headwall	
North Mowich Icefall	

Mowich Lake at nearly 5,000 feet in elevation is the largest lake in the park. It has become a popular destination because of its short yet scenic trails to Tolmie Peak Lookout and Spray Park. There is a ranger cabin on the south side and a free walk-in-only campground. The road to Mowich Lake usually doesn't open until late June, and frequently not until early July. Climbers should get their permits at the Park Service ranger station in Wilkeson; none are available at Mowich Lake.

The routes in this section top out on Liberty Cap (14,112 feet). To reach the true summit at Columbia Crest, climbers must travel nearly a mile, descending to the col at 13,600 feet before regaining the gentle slopes to 14,410 feet.

Carbon River approach: In this same general area, the Carbon River road goes to Ipsut Creek Campground, which offers climbers a way to approach routes on Liberty Wall, Liberty Ridge, Willis Wall, and Curtis Ridge. However, because it's often more practical to take on these routes from White River Campground, they are covered in the next section, on White River approaches. The Carbon River/Ipsut Creek approach provides quicker access to the routes, but the descent and return to the Ipsut Creek trailhead is unusually long. Some teams opt to approach from Ipsut Creek Campground and descend the Emmons/Winthrop Glaciers route to White River Campground. Climbers who want to start and end at the same trailhead prefer the White River Campground approach.

For the Carbon River approach to the Liberty/Willis/Curtis routes, take the 7.5-mile trail from Ipsut Creek Campground (2,300 feet) to Mystic Pass. Along the way, pass Carbon River Camp (2.9 miles from Ipsut Creek) and Dick Creek

Mowich Face
1. Edmunds Headwall
2. Central Mowich Face
3. North Mowich Headwall
4. North Mowich Icefall

Sunset Ridge

9,600 ft

9,200 ft

12,800 ft

Liberty Cap

12,500 ft

11,500 ft

Ptarmigan Ridge

exit gully

hourglass

North Mowich Glacier

North Mowich Icefall

to Mowich Lake

①
②
③
④

Camp (4 miles from Ipsut Creek). At Mystic Pass, just before the drop into Mystic Lake, ascend south along the climber's path through subalpine meadows up lower Curtis Ridge. Continue up the ridge to 7,200 feet, where the Carbon Glacier is best accessed. (For route details from this point, see the section on White River approaches.)

MOWICH FACE ROUTES

The Mowich Face possesses some of Mount Rainier's most dramatic alpine climbing. The face is shaped like a large triangle, 2 miles wide at the base and more than 4,000 feet high. With the apex at 13,600 feet, Sunset Ridge forms the southern side of the triangle, while Ptarmigan Ridge forms the northern side.

Climbing on the face can be characterized as long pitches of moderately steep snow and ice with some vertical rock bands. Climbers should be comfortable with constant exposure and short sections of steep ice and rock. Strong calves help. Belays and ice protection are called for, as any fall could prove catastrophic.

The best time to climb is in the early summer, when the approaches are direct, or in late fall, when the face turns icy and hard, making the climbing more challenging but the surface more stable. Mowich Face sees little climbing activity. Although the approach is long, the climbing is well worth it.

Getting to the Mowich Face and high camps: The approaches for these routes

Climbers high on the Central Mowich Face with the North Mowich Glacier far below. These routes are characterized by long, steep snow and ice pitches. © Mark Westman

Mowich Face
1. Sunset Ridge
2. Edmunds Headwall
3. Central Mowich Face
4. North Mowich Headwall
5. North Mowich Icefall

Liberty Cap

12,600 ft

12,500 ft

11,500 ft

Sunset Ridge

Edmunds Headwall

Edmunds Glacier

9,600 ft

10,200 ft

hourglass

exit gully

Ptarmigan Ridge

North Mowich Glacier

9,200 ft

To Mowich Lake

begin at Mowich Lake. From the lake, take the 3-mile trail to Spray Park, which slowly climbs through forest, past Eagles Roost Camp and Spray Falls, into the subalpine and alpine park. At the high point along the meadow trail, before the trail begins its descent toward the Carbon River, detour right and begin climbing the lower slopes of Ptarmigan Ridge.

Ascend gentle, open meadows to the small and stagnant Flett Glaciers. Continue up the ridge on snow or rock, passing between Echo Rock and Observation Rock. After passing Observation Rock, leave Ptarmigan Ridge at 8,300 feet and descend south for an elevation loss of 1,000 feet on 30- to 40-degree talus slopes to the North Mowich Glacier.

From 7,300 feet on the North Mowich Glacier, climb southwest on the glacier, negotiating icefalls and crevasses to the nunatak (rock protrusion in the glacier) at 9,200 feet, below the North Mowich Headwall. Here is a good bivy site for the **North Mowich Headwall** and **North Mowich Icefall** routes.

Climbers planning to ascend the **Edmunds Headwall** route or the **Central Mowich Face** route should continue traversing south on the North Mowich Glacier to another nunatak at 9,600 feet, below the central face.

Edmunds Headwall

The first of the Mowich Face routes to be climbed, the Edmunds Headwall is also considered the easiest and least hazardous route on the face. It ascends steep snow and ice slopes, never steeper than 55 degrees, to gain upper Sunset Ridge near 12,600 feet. Like the other headwall routes on Rainier, this climb is fun, airy, and direct. Before the Westside Road washed out, this route was best accessed from the St. Andrews Creek trailhead. With the road closure at Fish Creek, the Westside Road is no longer a faster approach, and climbers should approach from Mowich Lake.

> **ELEVATION GAIN:** 9,200 feet from Mowich Lake to Liberty Cap.
>
> **WHAT TO EXPECT:** Rockfall hazard; 40- to 55-degree snow and ice slopes. Grade III.
>
> **TIME:** 2 to 3 days; 6 to 8 hours from high camp to Liberty Cap. Carry over.
>
> **SEASON:** May, June, July, and October.
>
> **FIRST ASCENT:** John Rupley, Don Claunch, Fred Beckey, Tom Hornbein, and Herb Staley; June 23, 1957.
>
> **HIGH CAMP:** Between 8,800 and 10,000 feet near the base of the face. Look for protection from rock and ice that may fall from the face.

Ascend to the base of the wall on the Edmunds Glacier. Find the best location to cross the bergschrund somewhere around 9,600 feet, usually on the left side of the main Edmunds Headwall snow gullies. Begin climbing 30- to 40-degree

Across the Edmunds Glacier bergschrund, a climber begins the ascent of Mowich Face via the Edmunds Headwall.

snow or firn slopes. Climb directly up the face, bypassing rock bands through wide snow gullies. Virtually every major chute provides access to the snow and ice slopes above. At times, slope angle increases to 55 degrees and short patches of ice may be found.

Near 12,600 feet, the route connects with upper Sunset Ridge. There the angle decreases for the next few hundred feet as it continues along to 12,800 feet, where the ridge forces a leftward traverse onto the upper Mowich Face. Traverse steep ice, 50- to 55-degrees, and climb until the angle decreases above the Mowich Face apex at 13,500 feet. From there the angle continues to decrease as the route alternates along the ridge top and Liberty Cap Glacier to Liberty Cap. There may be crevasses above 13,600 feet on the Liberty Cap Glacier.

The Descent: Teams should carry over and descend the Emmons/Winthrop

Glaciers route (exiting at White River Campground) or descend the Tahoma Glacier and return to camp.

Descending the Tahoma Glacier makes for a long trip that may require significant routefinding. Descend the Tahoma to 8,500 feet on the Puyallup Cleaver and traverse north to the base of Sunset Ridge. Then climb to the 9,200-foot rock divide below the left arm of Sunset Ridge and traverse the upper Edmunds Glacier back to high camp, 6 to 10 hours.

Central Mowich Face

The second Mowich Face route to be climbed, the Central Mowich Face is a little longer and more committing than the Edmunds Headwall. This is another long and steep alpine classic, ascending the center of the Mowich Face triangle above the North Mowich Glacier. The route also offers a significant variation.

Expect moderately steep ice and snow, with the possibility of water ice and short sections of fourth-class rock. Although the pitches are not harder than

Leading out high on the Central Mowich Face © Eric Simonson

1. Central Mowich Face,
   exit variation
2. Central Mowich Face
3. North Mowich Headwall

upper Ptarmigan Ridge

12,700 ft
12,500 ft

upper
North Mowich
Headwall

12,000 ft

upper
Central Mowich
Face

what is found on the Edmunds Headwall, the route is precipitous and airy, with
fewer areas to take breaks. Additionally, the lower portion is exposed to the
hanging glacier on the Mowich Face. Speed and confidence on steep terrain
are necessary.

ELEVATION GAIN: 9,200 feet from Mowich Lake to Liberty Cap.

WHAT TO EXPECT: Rockfall and icefall hazards; 40- to 55-degree snow and
ice slopes. Grade III or IV.

TIME: 2 to 4 days; 6 to 9 hours from high camp to Liberty Cap. Carry over.

SEASON: May, June, July, and October.

FIRST ASCENT: Dee Molenaar, Gene Prater, Jim Wickwire, and Dick Pargeter;
July 24, 1966. Upper variation—Bill Cockerham, Ed Marquart, Bill Sumner,
and Del Young; July 4, 1967.

HIGH CAMP: A good bivy site can be found on the nunatak at 9,600 feet on
the North Mowich Glacier. Avoid camping near the face because of avalanche hazard.

Ascend the upper edge of the North Mowich Glacier toward the center of the
Mowich Face. Carry a few ice screws and pickets along. Cross the bergschrund
near 10,400 feet and begin climbing hard snow and ice slopes directly up the

face. This lower section of the route is exposed to significant ice and rock avalanches from the hanging glacier on Mowich Face; move quickly.

Angle left, climbing on 35- to 45-degree snow and ice slopes toward a prominent rock outcropping on the face near 11,500 feet. Staying left helps to avoid the hazards from the hanging glacier. From the rock outcropping, begin angling right on 45- to 55-degree ice slopes toward the rock bands above. Climb below and parallel to the three rock bands to 12,700 feet, where a short pitch of ice and rock (12 to 40 feet, depending on the year) gains access to the first snow ledge above the rock.

Continue left (north) along the narrow ledge as it drops slightly and turns an exposed corner to access an ice chute that climbs to upper Ptarmigan Ridge. The 45- to 55-degree ice chute climbs to the top of a glacier bulge over three pitches of steep ice. There is a rock band on the right. The grade decreases above the chute as the route climbs onto the broad crest of upper Ptarmigan Ridge. Ascend the glacier to Liberty Cap.

The route offers a Grade IV **upper variation.** From the rock band at 12,500 feet, continue ascending up and right, paralleling the rock band on your left. Bypass the rock bands on your left and ascend directly up the steep face to the apex of the Mowich Face. The angle is steep above the hanging glacier—50- to 60-degree ice slopes that relax where the Sunset and Ptarmigan Ridge routes meet at 13,500 feet. Bring ice screws; this variation is harder than the standard Mowich Face route. Finish by climbing Liberty Cap Glacier to Liberty Cap; watch for crevasses.

Descent: Teams should carry over and descend the Emmons/Winthrop Glaciers route (exiting at White River Campground) or descend the Tahoma Glacier and return to camp.

Descending the Tahoma Glacier makes for a long trip that may require significant routefinding. Descend the Tahoma to 8,500 feet on the Puyallup Cleaver and traverse north to the base of Sunset Ridge. Then climb to the 9,200-foot rock divide below the left arm of Sunset Ridge and traverse the upper Edmunds Glacier back to high camp, 6 to 10 hours.

North Mowich Headwall

Climbing the left side of the Mowich Face, the North Mowich Headwall ascends a hard line up the major northern ice slope to gain the crest of Ptarmigan Ridge. The climb has many technical sections that include vertical rock and ice both on the lower face and higher just below the crest of Ptarmigan Ridge. Bring ice screws and pickets for the route.

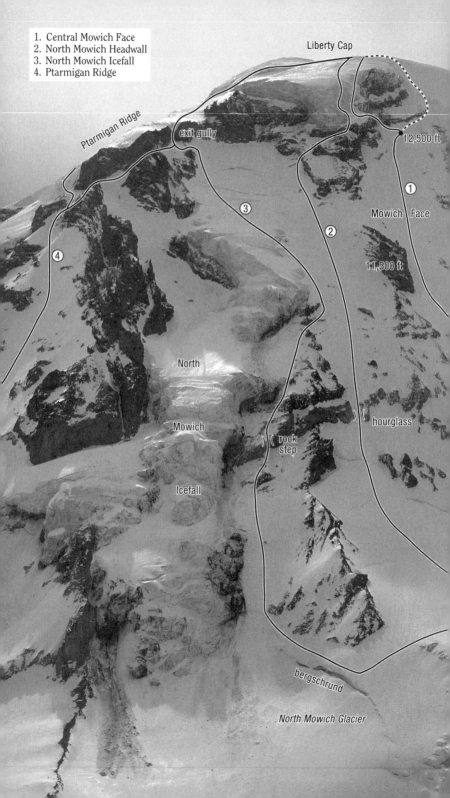

1. Central Mowich Face
2. North Mowich Headwall
3. North Mowich Icefall
4. Ptarmigan Ridge

Liberty Cap

Ptarmigan Ridge

exit gully

12,500 ft

③

①

Mowich Face

②

11,500 ft

④

North

Mowich

hourglass

) (rock
step

Icefall

bergschrund

North Mowich Glacier

At the time of its first ascent, the route was considered one of Rainier's hardest. Dan Davis, a member of the first-ascent team and a veteran of twenty-four routes on Rainier, considers this the best climb the mountain has to offer. The technical climbing and aesthetic values are high.

ELEVATION GAIN: 9,200 feet from Mowich Lake to Liberty Cap.

WHAT TO EXPECT: Rockfall and icefall hazards; 40- to 55-degree snow and ice slopes; fifth-class rock or easy aid. Grade IV.

TIME: 2 to 4 days; 6 to 10 hours from high camp to Liberty Cap. Carry over.

SEASON: May, June, July, and October.

FIRST ASCENT: Dan Davis, Mike Heath, Mead Hargis, and Bill Cockerham; July 22, 1968.

HIGH CAMP: A good bivy site can be found at 9,200 feet on the nunatak that divides the Edmunds and North Mowich Glaciers. Avoid camping near the headwall because of avalanche hazard.

Traverse and climb the North Mowich Glacier to the base of the Mowich Face, below the northern series of major snow and ice slopes. Cross the bergschrund near 10,000 feet and climb directly up snow to an hourglass in the first rock band. Climb through the short and difficult constriction on ice or rock; ice screws and a belay may be necessary.

Above the hourglass, ascend 40- to 45-degree snow or ice directly up the face to the rock bands below the ice cliff at 12,000 feet. Traverse up and right on the ledges to the narrowest rock band below the ice cliff and steep glacier. Climb through hard fifth-class rock (or A1 aid climbing) for 50 feet, gaining the top of the rock band. There a steep ice slope leads right, above the ice cliff. Ascend the 60-degree slope to gain upper Ptarmigan Ridge.

The angle now decreases, and the route finishes on the broad glacial crest of upper Ptarmigan Ridge and Liberty Cap Glacier to Liberty Cap; watch for crevasses.

Descent: Teams should carry over and descend the Emmons/Winthrop Glaciers route (exiting at White River Campground).

North Mowich Icefall

Climbing the far left edge of the Mowich Face, the North Mowich Icefall route actually parallels the icefall, ascending the extreme left of the Mowich Face to finish on upper Ptarmigan Ridge. Steep ice and short pitches of fifth-class rock are found, similar to the north Mowich Headwall; however, more rockfall has been noted, as much of this route lies below the cliffs of upper Ptarmigan Ridge. Bring ice screws and pickets for the route. Prolific climber Jim Wickwire, a member of the first-ascent team, confided that this route may be his personal favorite on Mount Rainier.

ELEVATION GAIN: 9,200 feet from Mowich Lake to Liberty Cap.

WHAT TO EXPECT: Rockfall and icefall hazard; 40- to 50-degree snow and ice slopes. Grade IV.

TIME: 2 to 4 days; 6 to 9 hours from high camp to Liberty Cap. Carry over.

SEASON: May, June, July, and October.

FIRST ASCENT: Jim Wickwire and Rob Schaller; June 26, 1970.

HIGH CAMP: A good bivy site can be found at 9,200 feet on the nunatak that divides the Edmunds and North Mowich Glaciers. Avoid camping near the headwall because of avalanche hazard.

Climb southeast around a rocky rib to the head of the North Mowich Glacier below the right side of the North Mowich Icefall. Traverse and stay above the bergschrund (near 9,000 feet) on steep 45-degree ice (possibly hard) and climb the snow gully that parallels the lowest section of the icefall. Rockfall and icefall is possible here, from the cliff bands and ice above.

Continue climbing up and right for several pitches to a 40-foot rock band. Climb on solid rock, fourth class, to gain another short snowfield. Climb it to another rock pitch that gains access to another broad snow slope. Continue upward and right, exiting the last snow slope below the icefall, 200 feet above the hourglass on the North Mowich Headwall route.

Continue up the extreme left side of the open snow face, paralleling the headwall route for 300 feet. Once the highest section of icefall is passed, diagonal left up the glacier to the narrowest exit gully in the cliff bands above. There may be a bergschrund at the top of the hanging glacier; expect hard snow or ice, 45 degrees.

At the exit gully, a vertical step in a narrow draw gains the upper Ptarmigan Ridge route. The gully is 5 to 15 feet long depending on the year, with solid rock; it may be verglassed. Climb through the gully onto Liberty Cap Glacier. There the slope angle decreases, with the route finishing along the broad glacial crest of upper Ptarmigan Ridge to Liberty Cap; watch for crevasses.

Descent: Teams should carry over and descend the Emmons/Winthrop Glaciers route (exiting at White River Campground).

PTARMIGAN RIDGE ROUTES

Principal climbing routes on Ptarmigan Ridge are the standard route with its two variations and the Ptarmigan Ice Cliff route. The ridge is consistently exciting and challenging, providing good climbing from start to finish.

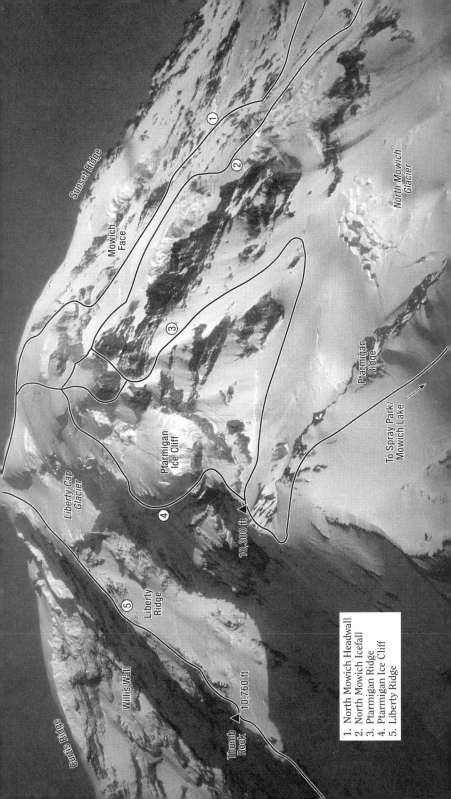

Sunset Ridge

Mowich Face

North Mowich Glacier

①

②

③

Ptarmigan Ridge

Ptarmigan Ice Cliff

To Spray Park/ Mowich Lake

④

10,300 ft

Liberty Cap Glacier

Liberty Ridge

⑤

Willis Wall

Curtis Ridge

Thumb Rock 10,760 ft

1. North Mowich Headwall
2. North Mowich Icefall
3. Ptarmigan Ridge
4. Ptarmigan Ice Cliff
5. Liberty Ridge

Getting to Ptarmigan Ridge and high camp: From Mowich Lake, take the 3-mile trail to Spray Park. At the high point along the meadow trail through the park, before the trail begins descending toward the Carbon River, detour right and begin climbing the lower slopes of Ptarmigan Ridge. Ascend gentle, open meadows to the small and stagnant Flett Glaciers. Continue up the ridge on snow or rock, passing between Echo Rock and Observation Rock. After passing Observation Rock, continue along the upper edge of the Russell Glacier, which gently falls to the left (east) while steep scree slopes fall to the North Mowich Glacier south of the Ptarmigan Ridge crest. The ridge narrows beyond 9,600 feet and crests near 10,300 feet, where there is an excellent bivy site.

Ptarmigan Ridge and Ice Cliff

Ptarmigan Ridge forms the impressive northwest flank of Mount Rainier. Adorned with tumbling glaciers and ice cliffs, the ridge is massive and broad, lacking the crested definition of other ridges. The climbs ascend moderate to steep snow and ice, with short sections of rock throughout. Bring ice screws and pickets. Above 10,300 feet, climbers take either the standard route (with a choice of two variations farther up) or the Ice Cliff route.

Many Pacific Northwest climbers consider Ptarmigan Ridge to be one of Mount Rainier's classics, rivaling even Liberty Ridge. Alex Bertulis, an accomplished Northwest climber with numerous Rainier ascents, calls it Washington state's preeminent alpine route.

ELEVATION GAIN: 9,200 feet from Mowich Lake to Liberty Cap.

WHAT TO EXPECT: Rockfall and icefall hazard; 40- to 55-degree snow and ice slopes; short sections of fifth-class climbing. Grade IV.

TIME: 2 to 4 days; 6 to 9 hours from high camp to Liberty Cap. Carry over.

SEASON: Spring through July.

FIRST ASCENT: Wolf Bauer and Jack Hossack; September 8, 1935. Second variation—Arnold Bloomer, Glenn Kelsey, Harold Pinsch, and Paul Williams; July 24th, 1966. Ice Cliff—Fred Beckey, John Rupley, and Herb Staley; August 5, 1956.

HIGH CAMP: A great bivy site exists at 10,300 feet on the ridge crest, before dropping to the 10,200-foot notch on the ridge.

For the **standard Ptarmigan Ridge route,** begin at the low notch on the ridge at 10,200 feet, then descend and traverse west for a quarter-mile onto the upper North Mowich Glacier. Move quickly; this area is subjected to significant icefall from the ice cliff above. Stay left as you descend until the lower rock buttress on Ptarmigan Ridge is cleared around 9,800 feet. Then turn left and cross the bergschrund to access a long diagonal snow slope that climbs up to

Liberty Cap

② Liberty Cap
Glacier

ice chute

exit gully

rock or ice

Ⓐ

Ⓑ

rock buttress
12,500 ft

rock or ice

Ptarmigan
Ridge

snow chute

①

1. Ptarmigan Ridge
   A. 1966 variation
   B. 1935 variation
2. Ptarmigan Ice Cliff,
   Liberty Wall finish

Close-up of Ptarmigan Ridge

1. Ptarmigan Ice Cliff
2. Liberty Wall Ice Cap

snow ramp

Liberty Cap Glacier

10,30
bivy

the left. Ascend this 40-degree snow slope leftward toward the rock cliffs above. Before reaching the cliffs, traverse left below the rock to access a steep 50-degree snow chute that leads straight up to the base of an upper rock buttress at around 12,500 feet.

From here, there are two popular variations. In the **first variation**, the first-ascent team turned left at the base of the upper buttress and traversed and climbed the steep 45- to 55-degree frozen snow and ice onto the Liberty Cap Glacier; take ice screws. Once on the glacier via this variation, continue up a steep ice chute between the icefall on the left and rock buttress on the right to gain the upper glacier dome. Find the best route through the seracs and crevasses on this section.

The **second variation** climbs to the right from the base of the upper buttress over fourth-class rock, icy and verglassed, to a chute between two rock bands. The chute continues over moderately steep terrain, 40- to 50- degrees, for two pitches until the right band gives way to the upper North Mowich Icefall. Shortly after, look for the exit gully on the left that provides access to upper Ptarmigan Ridge. The exit gully is a vertical step in a narrow draw, 5- to 15-

feet long, depending on the year. The rock is solid, but may be verglassed. After exiting the gully, regain the original line.

With either of these two variations, finish by ascending the broad glacial crest of upper Ptarmigan Ridge to Liberty Cap. Watch for crevasses on Liberty Cap Glacier.

For the **Ptarmigan Ice Cliff route,** begin at the Ptarmigan Ridge notch at 10,200 feet and climb to the base of the ice cliff on the east (left) side of the crest. Traverse and climb left on a sloping narrow ledge of black ice and glazed rock for 200 feet directly below the ice cliff. Move quickly because of severe icefall hazard. The ledge begins to broaden near the end of the ice cliff, where a steep snow/ice ramp cuts right and gains the Liberty Cap Glacier. Cut right and climb the ramp through the ice cliff to the heavily crevassed glacier above. Continue up the glacier, negotiating crevasses to reach Liberty Cap.

Descent: Carry over and descend the Emmons/Winthrop Glaciers or the Ingraham Direct/Disappointment Cleaver routes.

WHITE RIVER APPROACHES

Eleven routes and several variations cover much of Mount Rainier's north and northeast flank.

These climbs are categorized by proximity to lower Curtis Ridge or to Camp Schurman.

Lower Curtis Ridge routes	Camp Schurman routes
Liberty Wall Ice Cap	Winthrop Glacier and Russell Cliffs
Liberty Wall Direct	Emmons/Winthrop Glaciers
Liberty Ridge	
Willis Wall: Thermogenesis	
Willis Wall: West Rib	
Willis Wall: Central Rib	
Willis Wall: East Rib	
Willis Wall: East Willis Wall	
Curtis Ridge	

The two Camp Schurman routes are best approached from White River Campground. The campground is 5 miles beyond the White River Ranger Station, where climbers get permits.

The nine routes accessed via lower Curtis Ridge are approached from White River Campground, too, and thus are included in this section. But they can be approached also from Ipsut Creek Campground at the end of the Carbon River road.

It is also possible to approach the lower Curtis Ridge routes from Sunrise, up the road from White River Ranger Station. Sunrise has a visitor center, ranger station, gift shop, and snack grill. Although Sunrise appears to offer a 2,000-foot elevation advantage over the White River Campground, this is actually lost when time and energy are spent routefinding and traveling cross-country to make the most of the feet gained.

Many of the eleven routes in this section top out on Liberty Cap (14,112 feet). To reach the true summit at Columbia Crest, climbers must travel nearly a mile, descending to the col at 13,600 feet before regaining the gentle slopes to 14,410 feet.

LOWER CURTIS RIDGE ROUTES

The routes accessed from lower Curtis Ridge make up much of Mount Rainier's northern face. Many of them are considered Mount Rainier's hardest

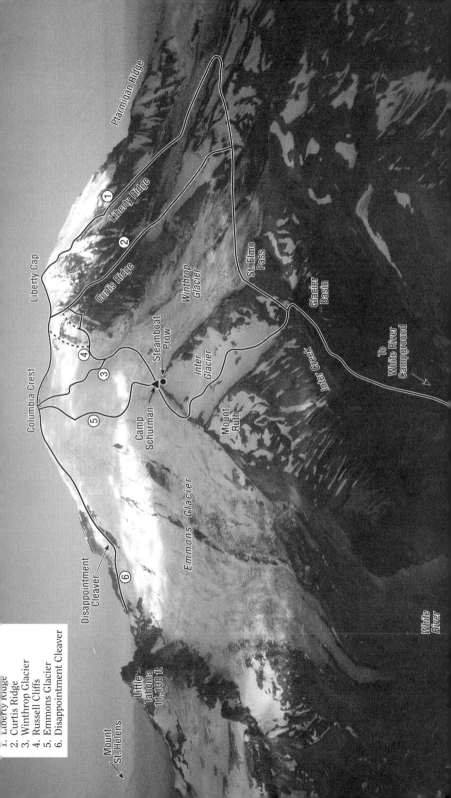

Mount
St. Helens

Little
Tahoma
11,138 ft

Disappointment
Cleaver

Emmons Glacier

6

Camp
Schurman

5

Columbia Crest

3

4

Steamboat
Prow

Liberty Cap

2

Curtis Ridge

Liberty Ridge

1

Ptarmigan Ridge

Winthrop
Glacier

Inter
Glacier

Mount
Ruth

St. Elmo
Pass

Glacier
Basin

Inter Creek

To
White River
Campground

White
River

1. Liberty Ridge
2. Curtis Ridge
3. Winthrop Glacier
4. Russell Cliffs
5. Emmons Glacier
6. Disappointment Cleaver

and most dangerous climbs. Lower Curtis Ridge is broad and sweeping, with gentle alpine slopes. Using the ridge, climbers can ascend to 7,200 feet and access the Carbon Glacier without the difficulties of negotiating the lower Carbon.

The entire north face, including **Liberty Wall, Liberty Ridge, Willis Wall, and Curtis Ridge,** is in full panoramic view from lower Curtis Ridge. Avalanches, waterfalls, and the jumbled Carbon Glacier are a few of the attractions. To the north lie Mount Baker and Glacier Peak and the city lights of Tacoma and Seattle spread out on the western horizon. The views are without doubt some of the most dramatic and spectacular on Mount Rainier.

Getting to lower Curtis Ridge: From White River Campground at 4,400 feet, follow the Glacier Basin trail 3.3 miles to Glacier Basin Camp at 6,000 feet. This trail is sometimes snow-covered till mid-June, but the path is wide and easy to follow. Glacier Basin is a popular and frequently filled camp for teams who elect to acclimatize and break the long day to Camp Schurman by stopping here first. Climbers headed to lower Curtis Ridge should attempt to cover more distance before setting up an intermediate camp.

From Glacier Basin, follow the climbers' path up the moraine toward the snout of the Inter Glacier, which lies in the southwest corner of the Inter Creek and Glacier Basin. The trail is not maintained, but a good social trail does exist. At approximately 6,600 feet, turn west (right) and ascend scree slopes to St. Elmo Pass (7,400 feet) and a possible bivy. From the pass, drop down to the Winthrop Glacier at 7,200 feet and traverse to lower Curtis Ridge. Most teams take 6 to 8 hours to reach lower Curtis Ridge from the White River parking lot. Traverse west on the broad ridge to 7,200 feet.

For the alternative **Carbon River approach** to lower Curtis Ridge, begin at Ipsut Creek Campground at the end of the Carbon River road in the northwest corner of the park. The Carbon River/Ipsut Creek approach provides quicker access to the routes, but the descent and return to the Ipsut Creek trailhead is unusually long. Some teams opt to approach from Ipsut Creek and descend the Emmons/Winthrop Glaciers route to the White River Campground. From Ipsut Creek Campground (2,300 feet), take the 7.5-mile trail to Mystic Pass. Along the way, pass Carbon River Camp (2.9 miles from Ipsut Creek) and Dick Creek Camp (4 miles from Ipsut Creek). At Mystic Pass, just before the drop into Mystic Lake, ascend south along the climber's path through subalpine meadows up lower Curtis Ridge. Continue up the ridge to 7,200 feet.

From 7,200 feet on Curtis Ridge, climbers headed for Liberty Wall, Liberty Ridge, or Willis Wall descend a snow and scree slope to access the Carbon Glacier. Getting to the Carbon from Curtis Ridge above 7,200 feet is difficult due to a very large cliff. Once on the Carbon Glacier, negotiate the crevasse systems and ascend the glacier to the intended route. The glacier becomes heavily

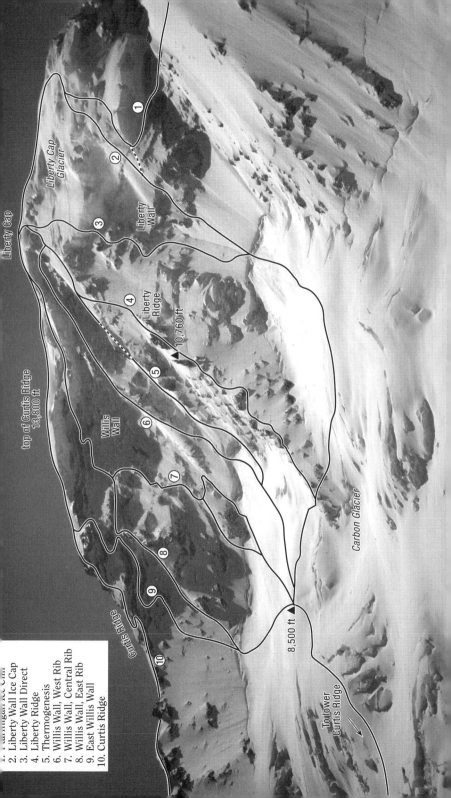

Liberty Cap Glacier

Liberty Cap

top of Curtis Ridge
13,800 ft

Liberty Wall

Willis Wall

Liberty Ridge

10,760 ft

Curtis Ridge

8,500 ft

Carbon Glacier

To lower
Curtis Ridge

1. Ptarmigan Ice Cliff
2. Liberty Wall Ice Cap
3. Liberty Wall Direct
4. Liberty Ridge
5. Thermogenesis
6. Willis Wall, West Rib
7. Willis Wall, Central Rib
8. Willis Wall, East Rib
9. East Willis Wall
10. Curtis Ridge

crevassed and very circuitous by mid-July. Climbers attempting Curtis Ridge simply stay on the ridge and start climbing upward.

These routes all share the same recommended descent: the Emmons/ Winthrop Glaciers route. Descend to Camp Schurman at 9,460 feet. From Camp Schurman, you can either climb over Steamboat Prow (fourth-class, loose rock) to the top of the Inter Glacier or descend the Emmons Glacier to Camp Curtis (9,000 feet), carrying over the ridge to the Inter Glacier. Descend the Inter Glacier to Glacier Basin and hike out the Glacier Basin Trail. Climbers usually take 5 to 10 hours from summit to trailhead. Teams climbing Liberty or Willis Wall may prefer to descend Liberty Ridge.

Liberty Wall: The Ice Cap and Direct

Liberty Wall lies between Liberty and Ptarmigan Ridges. The wall is reminiscent of Willis Wall—moderately steep and terribly dangerous; in fact, the Liberty Wall routes may be the most dangerous on Mount Rainier. Rockfall and icefall are common from the Liberty Cap Glacier and the rock cliffs above. Overall, the two principal routes on Liberty Wall—the Ice Cap route and the Direct route—are similar to Willis Wall, with hard ice prevalent because of the numerous avalanches that clean the face. The routes are characterized by 40- to 55-degree ice slopes and gullies. The Liberty Wall Direct requires climbers to surmount the ice cliff, which may require near-vertical ice climbing for one pitch. The climbing would be great, if the ice cliff weren't so active. These routes are for fast, slightly crazy, and ambitious climbers.

ELEVATION GAIN: 9,700 feet from White River Campground to Liberty Cap (or 11,800 feet from Ipsut Creek Campground to Liberty Cap).

WHAT TO EXPECT: Rockfall and icefall hazards; 40- to 50-degree snow and ice, a vertical pitch on the direct route. Grade IV or V.

TIME: 2 to 5 days; 8 to 10 hours from high camp to Liberty Cap. Carry over.

SEASON: May, June, and October.

FIRST ASCENT: Ice Cap—Paul Myhre, Don Jones, and Roger Oborn; June 30, 1968. Direct—Dusan Jagersky and Gary Isaacs; September 20, 1971.

HIGH CAMP: On the Carbon Glacier between Liberty and Ptarmigan Ridges at 8,500 feet, away from the wall. The site provides great access to the route and allows climbers to scope the wall prior to the ascent.

Liberty Wall Ice Cap: Ascend the Carbon Glacier to the headwall between Ptarmigan and Liberty Ridges. Cross the bergschrund and climb a 40-degree snow slope (ice in late season) up and to the right. Head to the snow gullies that access a second snow/ice slope, below the ice cliff. Ascend these gullies (45 degrees) and climb the second snow/ice slope toward the rock bands below the exit ramp in the ice cliff. (For a variation from the standard route, it is possible to cut right,

Liberty Cap

Liberty Cap Glacier

13,000 ft

Ptarmigan Ridge

Black Pyramid

ice cliff

①

④

Liberty Wall

ice cliff

Liberty Ridge

②

,760 ft

③

Thumb Rock

1. Ptarmigan Ice Cliff
2. Liberty Wall Ice Cap
3. Liberty Wall Direct
4. Liberty Ridge

Carbon Glacier

above these gullies, and finish via the Ptarmigan Ice Cliff route.) Mixed climbing ascends the rock bands and gains the exit ramp. Climb the ramp onto Liberty Cap Glacier. Continue up the glacier, negotiating crevasses to reach Liberty Cap.

Liberty Wall Direct: Ascend the Carbon Glacier to the headwall between Ptarmigan and Liberty Ridges. Cross the bergschrund and climb a 45-degree snow slope (ice in late season) up and to the left. Continue up through a series of small rock bands and snow chutes to the base of the ice cliff. Climb the ice cliff. It changes from year to year, but teams can expect a difficult ice-climbing lead with belays to gain Liberty Cap Glacier above. (The first-ascent party used ten ice screws.) Once above the ice cliff, negotiate crevasses and continue to Liberty Cap.

Descent: Carry over and descend the Emmons/Winthrop Glaciers route to Camp Schurman.

Liberty Ridge

Featured in *Fifty Classic Climbs of North America* (by Steve Roper and Allen Steck, Sierra Club, 1996), Liberty Ridge is truly the celebrated mountaineering classic of Rainier. The 5,500-foot ridge splits the steep north faces of Willis Wall and Liberty Wall, providing moderately difficult and protected climbing to the summit. This committing climb can only be accessed by crossing the jumbled ice and crevasses of the 900-foot-deep Carbon Glacier.

The exposed ridge challenges climbers with moderate to steep ice climbing and a perched bivy at Thumb Rock. Willis and Liberty Walls are the backdrops that provide a constant showcase of ice avalanches and rockfall from the summit ice cap. Since the climb is so long and committing, climbers must plan their trip well, usually needing to carry their gear to the summit and descend another route.

> **ELEVATION GAIN:** 9,700 feet from White River Campground to Liberty Cap (or 11,800 feet from Ipsut Creek Campground to Liberty Cap).
>
> **WHAT TO EXPECT:** Rockfall and icefall hazard; 55-degree ice slopes; glacier travel. Grade III or IV.
>
> **TIME:** 2 to 4 days; most parties need 2 days to reach the Thumb Rock high camp (10,760); 5 to 10 hours from high camp to Liberty Cap. Carry over.
>
> **SEASON:** May to mid-July.
>
> **FIRST ASCENT:** Ome Daiber, Arnie Campbell, and Jim Borrow; September 30, 1935.
>
> **INTERMEDIATE CAMP:** Lower Winthrop Glacier (7,200 feet), lower Curtis Ridge (7,200 feet), or Carbon Glacier (7,200 to 8,500 feet).
>
> **HIGH CAMP:** Thumb Rock (10,760 feet).

Liberty Ridge can be gained on the Willis Wall side (east) or the Liberty Wall side (west). Then climb the west side of the ridge crest, ascending moderate

1. Ptarmigan Ice Cliff
2. Liberty Wall Ice Cap
3. Liberty Wall Direct
4. Liberty Ridge
5. Thermogenesis
6. Willis Wall, West Rib
7. Willis Wall, Central Rib

Liberty Cap

of Curtis Ridge
13,800 ft

Traverse of Angels

Liberty Cap
Glacier

West Rib

13,000 ft

Thermogenesis

Black
Pyramid

Willis
Wall

④

⑦

⑥

⑤

④

Thumb
Rock
10,760 ft

Liberty
Wall

③

①

②

,500 ft

Carbon Glacier

snow and scree slopes (30 to 40 degrees) to Thumb Rock (10,760 feet), a large gendarme composed of questionable rock. The saddle just on the uphill side of this prominent rock formation provides an excellent high camp. The area is small, however, and can be crowded on busy weekends. Also note that falling rock from Thumb Rock is possible.

From Thumb Rock, choose one of three short variations to gain the ridge above the rock face behind camp. The east face variation on the Willis Wall side is a moderate snow slope staying close to the rock. It gains the ridge 400 feet above camp and is exposed. The right-center gully is the steepest variation, having a 15-foot ice pitch (70 to 80 degrees) in a narrow gully that runs out onto the ridge directly above the rock. The west face variation on the Liberty Wall side is also a moderate snow slope with exposure.

Once the ridge crest is regained, ascend 40- to 50-degree snow and ice slopes to the base of the Black Pyramid at 12,400 feet. Then traverse toward Willis Wall and climb the open face. This is the steepest part of the climb, sometimes 55 degrees. It runs for three or four rope lengths and can be hard and icy, particularly near the top of the Black Pyramid. Climb to the crest of the ridge above the Black Pyramid, where the slope angle decreases and the route joins Liberty Cap Glacier at 13,000 feet.

From there, ascend moderately steep glaciated slopes toward the bergschrund directly above. Depending on the year and season, the bergschrund may require a short section (10 to 40 feet) of vertical ice climbing to surmount, or it may simply involve end-running the obstacle. Above the bergschrund, the route continues on the glacier for the last few hundred feet of elevation gain to Liberty Cap.

Descent: Carry over and descend the Emmons/Winthrop Glaciers route to Camp Schurman.

ROUTES ON THE WILLIS WALL

If Mount Rainier has one noted and feared place, it is the Willis Wall on the northern face. The massive wall begins at 9,600 feet and rises 4,000 feet steeply over snow, ice, rock, and frozen volcanic mud and ash to the summit ice cap. The wall has three ribs or incipient ridges—the west, central, and east ribs—and they offer the least hazardous lines up the main wall by avoiding avalanche/ice chutes. Although the climbing is not any steeper than on many of Rainier's other hard routes, this wall shouts danger. Climbers considering these routes should begin with a good assessment of the dangers and be prepared for hardship, fear, physical strain, and constant objective hazards.

The primary consideration is speed. Towering above much of the wall is a 200- to 300-foot ice cliff that randomly releases avalanches of ice and rock that sweep the face. A good portion of the wall can be swept by a large avalanche at any time without notice. Other hazards include small slides of snow and rock that frequent the gullies. Willis Wall is committing, once on route. The only possible escapes require a long and exposed traverse to Liberty Ridge or Curtis Ridge. Couple these considerations with the fact that climbers can't see incoming weather from the south, and the Willis Wall proves to be some of Mount Rainier's most hazardous terrain.

Consider climbing Willis Wall only under ideal conditions that include a few days of cold weather with no precipitation preceding the climb. The cold days should help rocks and snow adhere to the wall. Assessing the wall prior to the climb is of great benefit, too. Consider this an opportunity to check the activity of the summit ice cliff and to get an overall sense for what's going on. Some teams ascend the wall unroped in the interests of faster progress. The ability to move fast, and a familiarity with moderate ice and rocky terrain with intense exposure, is mandatory. If roping up, bring a few pickets, ice screws, and some pitons for protection.

Of the Willis Wall climbers I interviewed, not one mentioned the views, aesthetic values, or quality climbing features of the routes. Their predominant concerns and comments revolved around the ominous ice cliff, frozen rock slab ledges, and frequency of small debris avalanches in the gullies.

Getting to Willis Wall: From 7,200 feet on Curtis Ridge, descend a snow and scree slope to the Carbon Glacier. (Avoid going too high onto Curtis Ridge, because it quickly becomes a large cliff and denies access to the Carbon.) Once on the glacier, negotiate the crevasse systems and ascend toward Willis Wall. The glacier is heavily crevassed and very circuitous by mid-July. Select only a campsite that is well away from the wall and from the possibility of being destroyed by an avalanche. Large avalanches may travel as much as a mile or more out from the base.

Willis Wall: Thermogenesis

This long couloir on the west side of Willis Wall separates the wall from Liberty Ridge. The first-ascent party climbed the couloir by mistake while searching for the West Rib in the dark. After ascending the couloir for a bit, they noticed their mistake and quickly completed the climb. Occasional small slides of loose, pebbly debris were reported, and the entire route was swept twice the following day by avalanches.

Liberty Cap

To Columbia Crest ⟶

13,800 ft

Black Pyramid

Thumb Rock 10,760 ft

Liberty Ridge

Willis Wall

Carbon Glacier

Curtis Ridge

1. Liberty Ridge
2. Thermogenesis
3. Willis Wall, West Rib
4. Willis Wall, Central Rib
5. Willis Wall, East Rib
6. East Willis Wall

The route is actually an ice chute that is frequently dumped upon by the ice cliff above. The route tops out at about 13,500 feet, where it joins the upper Liberty Ridge route. Of all the routes on Willis Wall, Thermogenesis is the most hazardous.

ELEVATION GAIN: 9,700 feet from White River Campground to Liberty Cap (or 11,800 feet from Ipsut Creek Campground to Liberty Cap).

WHAT TO EXPECT: Serious rockfall and icefall hazard; sustained 35- to 55-degree snow and ice slopes, with one short 60-degree section. Grade III-IV.

TIME: 3 to 5 days; 5 to 7 hours from high camp to the upper Black Pyramid on Liberty Ridge. Liberty Ridge descent to high camp, 5 hours from Liberty Cap; or carry over.

SEASON: Winter through May.

FIRST ASCENT: Steve Doty, Jerome Eberharter, and Jon Olson; May 20, 1978.

HIGH CAMP: The Carbon Glacier, away from the wall, below 8,500 to 9,000 feet.

Climb the Carbon Glacier to 9,800 feet toward the far western couloir of the Willis Wall. Cross the bergschrund on the large debris cone of snow and ice and climb the 30- to 50-degree firn snow and ice slopes. The steepest section is in the hourglass one third of the way up the couloir, where a short section of 60-degree ice is found. Near 12,500 feet and directly below the giant ice cliff, the couloir diagonals right to gain upper Liberty Ridge.

Some reprieve from the danger is offered once climbers reach the steep Black Pyramid pitch on Liberty Ridge (see route description for Liberty Ridge). The slope angle decreases above the Black Pyramid, on the crest of Liberty Ridge as the route joins Liberty Cap Glacier. In some years, the bergschrund requires a short, vertical ice climb to access the glacier above. Continue to Liberty Cap.

Descent: Descend Liberty Ridge, or carry over and descend the Emmons/Winthrop Glaciers route to Camp Schurman.

Willis Wall: West Rib

This rib is a protrusion broad and snowy at its base, crested and somewhat protected in the middle, and broad with exposed rocky cliff bands for the last 500 feet below the ice cliff. Any protection offered is actually just a token, because large rib-sweeping avalanches and slides are possible.

The most hazardous sections are at the points where you access and exit the crested rib. The exit requires traversing onto a broad face of narrow terraced ledges below the ice cliff. Climber Alex Bertulis said that less than 5 minutes after he and Jim Wickwire crossed under the ice cliff, a large serac broke free and swept part of the route.

ELEVATION GAIN: 9,700 feet from White River Campground to Liberty Cap (or 11,800 feet from Ipsut Creek Campground to Liberty Cap).

WHAT TO EXPECT: Serious rockfall and icefall hazard; 35- to 55-degree rock, snow, and ice slopes with traversing. Grade IV or V.

TIME: 3 to 5 days; 6 to 8 hours from high camp to upper Liberty Ridge. Liberty Ridge descent to high camp, 5 hours from Liberty Cap; or carry over.

SEASON: Winter and spring.

FIRST ASCENT: Charlie Bell; June 12, 1961. First winter ascent—Alex Bertulis and Jim Wickwire; February 11, 1970.

HIGH CAMP: The Carbon Glacier, away from the wall, below 8,500 feet.

Ascend the Carbon Glacier toward the base of the Willis Wall's far western couloir (start of the Thermogenesis route) and a possible location to cross the bergschrund, 9,800 feet. Once across, climb and traverse left out of the gully and onto the broad lower cleaver.

Continue up a frozen snowfield toward the narrowing crest (easy 30 to 35 degrees). A 60-foot section of rock requires fourth-class climbing to gain snow ramps that lead to the crest of the rib. Ascend the rib, bypassing any rock bands below and to the left through moderate snow ramps that regain the crest.

Climb the rib crest to the last buttress. Bypass that buttress on the left over short snow and rock bands to gain an upper terraced ledge below the ice cliff. Climb that ledge up and right to the corner below the ice cliff. Climbing the icy ledge and rounding the corner is considered the most difficult. After the corner (with the ice cliff still above), traverse onto the steep, open face that leads to upper Liberty Ridge. A short rappel may be needed to get on Liberty Ridge. Climb onto the Liberty Cap Glacier, crossing the bergschrund near 13,700 feet. Continue to Liberty Cap.

Descent: Descend Liberty Ridge, or carry over and descend the Emmons/Winthrop Glaciers route to Camp Schurman.

Willis Wall: Central Rib

Heavily buttressed, the Central Rib ascends terrain similar to the West Rib. However, it requires more traversing to avoid rock bands that block the rib crest. The rib is more of a face and gully climb than a climb of a crested rib, and this proves circuitous and time-consuming.

The story of a tough Central Rib ascent in May 1971 gives a flavor of the possible hazards of a Willis Wall route. Climbing in hard, icy conditions, Eddie

Liberty Cap

ice cliff

Traverse of Angels

ice cliff

5

last
buttress

13,000 ft

Black
Pyramid

1

3

4

2

gray buttress
11,000 ft

hourglass

1. Liberty Ridge
2. Thermogenesis
3. Willis Wall, West Rib
4. Willis Wall, Central Rib
5. Willis Wall, East Rib

large
buttress

Boulton and Jim Wickwire were forced to bivouac on the wall near 13,000 feet in a storm. They sought shelter in a protected moat/cave as avalanches swept its entrance throughout the night. When the weather did not relent the next day, they forced their way through deep snow to Liberty Cap, where they endured another desperate snow-cave bivouac. Eventually, 7 days after leaving the trailhead at Ipsut Creek, they made it down to the highway near White River Ranger Station. Wickwire says the experience of those bivouacs and others like them on Rainier were critical to his later survival near the summit of K2.

ELEVATION GAIN: 9,700 feet from White River Campground to Liberty Cap (or 11,800 feet from Ipsut Creek Campground to Liberty Cap).

WHAT TO EXPECT: Serious rockfall and icefall hazard; 35- to 55-degree rock, snow, and ice slopes with traversing. Grade IV or V.

TIME: 3 to 5 days; 7 to 10 hours from high camp to Liberty Cap. Liberty Ridge descent to high camp, 5 hours from Liberty Cap; or carry over.

SEASON: Winter through June.

FIRST ASCENT: Paul Dix and Dean Caldwell; June 20, 1965.

HIGH CAMP: The Carbon Glacier, away from the wall, below 8,500 feet.

The Central Rib begins against the Carbon Glacier as a large buttress that blocks direct access. Gain the wall by crossing the bergschrund on large snow-deposition cones to the left or right of the buttress, 9,800 feet. Ascend frozen snow or ice to terraced ledges that give access to the rib crest. Climbers have reported a barrage of hail-size rock and ice until the rib crest was gained. Then ascend the rib, bypassing four arch-like rock bands by moving below and to the left on steep snow traverses and gullies.

After the fourth arch, climb snow slopes right of the crest for a few hundred feet to a crumbly gray buttress overhead. Traverse left when feasible and gain the top of the gray buttress via an open snow slope. Above this buttress, ascend left toward a short, narrow snow or ice chute that leads to a rightward traverse on slab rock or verglas. Ascend the slab rock to a steep snow and rock cliff—a "frosty cliff"—where a 40-foot traverse on difficult rock provides access to an easy 20-foot vertical cliff that tops out on the rib crest. Continue scrambling up moderate snow slopes, joining the original East Rib route, and proceed about three rope lengths to the steep rock that forms the base of the ice cliffs.

The ice cliffs rest on three terraced rock bands. Climb steep, frozen conglomerate consisting of rock and mud for 150 feet (fourth-class climbing) to a ledge. Traverse right on the short, exposed ledge for 15 feet to a short fifth-class step that gains the second of the terraced ledges. From the second ledge, traverse and climb 40 feet to a narrow, exposed ledge and blind corner. Turn the corner (possible verglas or snow) and climb 20 feet to easier snow slopes that reach the exit ramp between the ice cliffs. This traverse—the Traverse of Angels—is airy; belays and protection are difficult to place. Once the summit plateau is reached above the ice cliff, climb west on gentle glacier slopes to Liberty Cap.

Descent: Descend Liberty Ridge, or carry over and descend the Emmons/ Winthrop Glaciers route to Camp Schurman.

Willis Wall: East Rib

The East Rib was the first of the Willis Wall ribs to be climbed. The rib is actually a series of buttresses—less defined on the lower third of the wall, prominent on the second third, then nonexistent as the rib flattens for the last third to exit between the ice cliffs. The route follows the rock buttresses for two-thirds of the way up the wall. Although a longer and less direct route than the other two Willis Wall ribs, the crest of the East Rib offers some protection from the ice cliff and rockfall hazards above. Higher on the buttressed

A climber traverses steep, icy snow from the top of the East Rib to the Central Rib of the Willis Wall. Note ice cliffs above. © *Jim Wickwire*

rib, however, climbers must commit to a long rightward traverse below the ice cliff—or else exit left to upper Curtis Ridge, a much safer option.

ELEVATION GAIN: 9,700 feet from White River Campground to Liberty Cap (or 11,800 feet from Ipsut Creek Campground to Liberty Cap).

WHAT TO EXPECT: Serious rockfall and icefall hazard; 35- to 55-degree rock, snow, and ice slopes with traversing. Grade IV or V.

TIME: 3 to 5 days; 7 to 10 hours from high camp to Liberty Cap. Liberty Ridge descent to high camp, 5 hours from Liberty Cap; or carry over.

SEASON: Winter through June.

FIRST ASCENT: Dave Mahre, Fred Dunham, Jim Wickwire, and Don Anderson; June 8, 1963.

HIGH CAMP: The Carbon Glacier, away from the wall, below 8,500 feet.

Climb the Carbon Glacier to the eastern edge of the wall, left of the small lower East Rib rock outcroppings. Cross the bergschrund on a deposition cone and climb snow slopes to the crest of the first main rock buttress on the rib. Rockfall from upper Curtis Ridge is likely here; protection is offered once on the crest.

Climb the rib and arc right to the crest of a second buttress; then continue toward the final and largest buttress, which lies 1,500 to 1,700 feet above the Carbon Glacier. A 75-foot section of loose and very steep rock must be climbed to gain the crest of the largest buttress, or eastern rib. From the crest of the largest buttress, climb on snow and rock to the head of the rib crest, at about 12,200 feet. (An exit variation is possible from this point; see below.) A prominent terraced snow ledge to the right must be traversed. The long traverse on the snow ledge is exposed to the ice cliffs and therefore hard and icy. Traverse the ledge to where the East Rib and Central Rib routes join. Now proceed about three rope lengths to the steep rock that forms the base of the ice cliffs.

The ice cliffs rest on three terraced rock bands. Climb steep, frozen conglomerate consisting of rock and mud for 150 feet (fourth-class climbing) to a ledge. Traverse right on the short, exposed ledge for 15 feet to a short fifth-class step that gains the second of the terraced ledges. From the second ledge, traverse and climb 40 feet to a narrow, exposed ledge and blind corner. Turn the corner (possible verglas or snow) and climb 20 feet to easier snow slopes that reach the exit ramp between the ice cliffs. This traverse—the Traverse of Angels—is airy; belays and protection are difficult to place. Once the summit plateau is reached above the ice cliff, climb west on gentle glacier slopes to Liberty Cap.

Exit variation: From the head of the rib crest where the snow ledge leads

Top of Curtis Ridge
13,800 ft

Columbia Crest

ice cliff

To Liberty
Cap

Traverse of Angels

snow
ramp

exit
gullies

Curtis Ridge

traverse

bypass

12,200 ft

traverse ledge

2

3

Willis
Wall

1

largest
buttress

gray
buttress
11,000 ft

second
buttress

first
buttress

1. Willis Wall, Central Rib
2. Willis Wall, East Rib
3. East Willis Wall
4. Curtis Ridge

to a rightward traverse, climb to the left instead. You can then ascend moderate snow, ice, and rock to finish the climb on the upper East Willis Wall route (class 4) to exit on upper Curtis Ridge.

Descent: Descend Liberty Ridge, or carry over and descend the Emmons/Winthrop Glaciers route to Camp Schurman.

Willis Wall: East Willis Wall

The least hazardous of the Willis Wall routes, this climb stays east of the three major ribs and avoids much of the exposure to the ice cliff above. Skirting along the eastern flank of Willis Wall, the route ascends a series of snowfields, chutes, ledges, and short rock bands to finish through the exit gullies of upper Curtis Ridge. Although the ice cliff is not as threatening, the route still exposes climbers to extensive rockfall from upper Curtis Ridge. The first-ascent party chose this route after a number of ice-cliff avalanches swept the route they had intended to ascend on the wall.

ELEVATION GAIN: 9,700 feet from White River Campground to Liberty Cap (or 11,800 feet from Ipsut Creek Campground to Liberty Cap).

WHAT TO EXPECT: Rockfall and icefall hazards; 35- to 55-degree rock, snow, and ice slopes with traversing. Grade IV.

TIME: 3 to 5 days; 7 to 10 hours from high camp to Liberty Cap. Liberty Ridge descent to high camp, 5 hours from Liberty Cap; or carry over.

SEASON: Winter through June.

FIRST ASCENT: Ed Cooper and Mike Swayne; June 26, 1962.

HIGH CAMP: The Carbon Glacier, away from the wall, below 8,500 feet.

Climb to the head of the Carbon Glacier, left of the Willis Wall, East Rib. Cross the bergschrund and climb the western flank of Curtis Ridge via uneventful 30- to 45-degree snow slopes through rock bands that require scrambling. A series of snow ledges and ramps climb to the base of a major rock cliff above (near 11,000 feet). There, another key snow/ice ledge leads right on a long traverse to bypass the major rock cliff. That ledge ends in a broken rock band. Ascend the rock band, actually a steep fourth-class boulder field with very loose rocks, to the snow slopes above. Climb carefully; significant rockfall is possible.

From the top of the boulderfield, climb a series of moderate snow and rock ramps—first to the right, then to the left—to the final snow tongue from upper Curtis Ridge, at 13,300 feet. Continue along the snow crest to the top of Curtis Ridge at 13,800 feet. From here, you can either cross the broad summit col south to the crater rim and Columbia Crest, or traverse gentle glacier slopes west to Liberty Cap.

Descent: Descend Liberty Ridge, or carry over and descend the Emmons/ Winthrop Glaciers route to Camp Schurman.

Curtis Ridge

Curtis Ridge is the largest and most prominent of Mount Rainier's northern ridges, dividing the Willis Wall and Carbon Glacier on the west from the Winthrop Glacier on the east. The lower ridge is broad at the base, narrowing as it ascends to an apex at 10,300 feet, where the technical climbing begins.

Years of unsuccessful attempts and a fatality in 1969 led many climbers to regard this route as a rockfall death trap. Climbers in later years reported the route to be less dangerous than originally perceived and called the rock quite solid by Mount Rainier standards. In any case, an early start with fast climbing means a safer ascent. Curtis Ridge is a hard classic that demands good skills in routefinding, rock climbing, and snow climbing.

> **ELEVATION GAIN:** 9,700 feet from White River Campground to Liberty Cap (or 11,800 feet from Ipsut Creek Campground to Liberty Cap).
>
> **WHAT TO EXPECT:** Rockfall and icefall hazard; 35- to 55-degree snow and ice slopes with traversing; fifth-class rock and A2 aid climbing. Grade IV.
>
> **TIME:** 3 to 5 days; 6 to 8 hours from high camp to the top of Curtis Ridge at 13,800 feet. Carry over.
>
> **SEASON:** Winter through June.
>
> **FIRST ASCENT:** Gene Prater and Marcel Schuster; July 21, 1957.
>
> **HIGH CAMP:** There is an excellent bivy ledge on the east side of the Curtis Ridge crest, 200 feet before a prominent rock gendarme at 10,200 feet. You can also bivy at the base of the gendarme.

From 7,200 feet on Curtis Ridge, climb on gradually steeper and more avalanche-prone snow slopes to the apex of the ridge at 10,300 feet. At this point, traverse the crest until you reach a 200-foot-deep notch in the ridge. Here, descend the west side of the ridge approximately 100 feet on loose rock or snow to a rappel station. Rappel 70 feet to the snow or loose rock ledge, below and west of the notch and ridge crest.

Continue along for roughly 300 yards, staying on the crest of the ridge when possible. Vertical steps along the ridge crest can be bypassed on either side without major difficulty. There is an excellent site for high camp on the east side of the ridge crest at 10,200 feet, about 200 feet before the prominent rock gendarme, where another small bivy site exists. Pass the gendarme on the left (east), then traverse to the Willis Wall side of the crest and climb to the first major rock band.

From here, there are a couple of options to gain the snowfield above the

exit gullies

second snowfield

first snowfield

aid crack

bypass

rock gendarme

Photo taken from the bivy site at 10,200 feet © Sanderson/ Steiger Collection

first rock band. The first option is an open-book, 75-foot A2 crack that lies straight ahead west of the ridge crest and provides direct access to the snow-field above. Negotiating this obstacle is time-consuming.

The other option is to climb and traverse to the right, below the rock band, on a series of snow steps that lead to a small snow slope. Continue climbing up, looking for a snow ledge that traverses downward and to the left. Traverse to the end of this ledge, where 10 to 15 feet of easy third-class climbing provides access to the snowfield above the first rock band. Take small chocks (half-inch to 1.5 inches) and pickets for rock or snow protection along both the right and left traverses.

At the snowfield, climb up and leftward on firn snow to a small rock band, passing by it to get to the second major rock band. Bypass this second major band by traversing a snow/ice slope to the right, where a 20- to 30-foot section of third-class rock gains access to the second firn snowfield. From here, traverse up and leftward to the exit gullies.

The gullies are straightforward. Several small rock bands must be passed in the gullies, and they require either fifth-class climbing or mixed climbing depending on conditions. Above the rock bands, gain the Curtis Ridge snow dome. Continue along the easy snow crest to the top of Curtis Ridge at 13,800 feet. From here, you can either cross the broad summit col south to the crater rim and Columbia Crest, or traverse gentle glacier slopes west to Liberty Cap.

Descent: Carry over and descend the Emmons/Winthrop Glaciers route to Camp Schurman.

CAMP SCHURMAN ROUTES

Camp Schurman high camp provides the best access for the **Winthrop Glacier/Russell Cliffs** route and for the **Emmons/Winthrop Glaciers** route. Camp Schurman sits at the base of Steamboat Prow—where two ridges merge from below into a triangle that divides the largest glaciers on Rainier, the Emmons and Winthrop. The Inter Glacier fills the recess between the ridges on the backside of Steamboat Prow.

At 9,460 feet, Camp Schurman is Rainier's second-most popular high camp, after Camp Muir. Camp Schurman has a ranger hut and outhouse. On the northeast side of Rainier, the camp enjoys great sunrises of pink and gold. Little Tahoma—at 11,138 feet, Washington's third-highest peak—lies to the southeast of the camp, while the urban glow of the Puget Sound region illuminates the northwestern horizon after sunset.

Climbers spending the night will probably camp on the snowy edge of the Winthrop Glacier. Build sturdy camps and anchor everything well; Camp Schurman is noted for fierce, tent-destroying winds. Since glaciers flank camp, excellent opportunities to practice crevasse rescue or ice climbing are a stone's throw away.

Getting to high camp: Begin from White River Campground at 4,400 feet, taking the Glacier Basin trail 3.3 miles to Glacier Basin Camp at 6,000 feet.

Follow the climbers' path from the basin up the right side of the creek to the snout of the Inter Glacier at 6,800 feet, in the southwest corner of the valley. The Inter Glacier serves as a great training ground for inexperienced climbers.

Ascend the Inter Glacier, negotiating crevasses as needed to Camp Curtis (9,000 feet). This camp on the south side of Ruth Ridge can accommodate teams of four or fewer climbers. From Camp Curtis, traverse and descend 150 feet to the Emmons Glacier on a climbers' path of loose rock and clay. Rope up and ascend the glacier, paralleling the edge of Ruth Ridge to the base of Steamboat Prow and Camp Schurman (9,460 feet).

Another camp, Emmons Flats (9,800 feet), sits above Camp Schurman. Emmons Flats is entirely on the glacier, and those spending the night use the blue-bag waste disposal system.

Winthrop Glacier/Russell Cliffs

The Winthrop Glacier/Russell Cliffs route is rarely climbed. The Winthrop Glacier offers the same climbing terrain as the Emmons/Winthrop route: crevasses, icefalls, seracs, and snow bridges. It attracts teams who prefer routefinding and want to avoid the Emmons boot track.

Continuing the adventure, teams traverse into the large cirque above Russell Cliffs, with access to the steep gullies, faces, and buttresses of upper Curtis Ridge. Although the Russell Cliffs variations are not hard, they are exposed and intimidating. This is a route for teams looking for something unusual and wild in a summit climb from Camp Schurman.

ELEVATION GAIN: 10,000 feet from White River Campground to Columbia Crest.

WHAT TO EXPECT: Rockfall and icefall hazard; 45- to 50-degree snow and ice slopes; short rock steps on the central route; glacier travel. Grade II or III.

TIME: 2 to 3 days; 6 to 9 hours from Camp Schurman to the summit, 3 to 4 hours for descent to Camp Schurman.

SEASON: Spring through July.

FIRST ASCENT: Don Jones, Jim Kurtz, Dave Mahre, and Gene Prater; July 1960. Central bowl—Dean Bentley, Jim Springer, and John L. Thompson; July 8, 1973. Upper headwall—Chris Mahre, Dave Mahre, and Gene Prater; 1974.

HIGH CAMP: Camp Schurman (9,460 feet) or Emmons Flats (9,800 feet).

From Emmons Flats, head west onto the Winthrop Glacier. Traverse and climb through the cirque between the shoulders of the Emmons and Winthrop Glaciers. There are many large crevasses here, and teams should waste little time;

Columbia
Crest
col
13,600 ft
13,800 ft
Liberty Cap
③
②
①
Curtis
Ridge
Russell
Cliffs
Winthrop
Glacier

1. Russell Cliffs, gully, original ascent
2. Russell Cliffs, central bowl variation
3. Russell Cliffs, upper headwall variation

an active icefall heads the cirque. Negotiate the crevasses and ascend the raised shoulder of the Winthrop; depending on the year, you may encounter a short section of 60-degree ice.

Once on the shoulder, ascend moderate glacier slopes to between 12,000 and 12,500 feet. Find the best access into the large, open-face cirque above Russell Cliffs. From here, climbers have three options in ascending to upper Curtis Ridge.

The far-right gully is the original route and involves a long traverse. The cliffs below intensify the exposure in the 45-degree gully. Depending on the season, there may be a short rocky or verglassed section near the top before the gully exits to upper Curtis Ridge.

The central bowl variation is not as steep as the gully, but climbers must negotiate a small vertical rock band to exit the cirque onto upper Curtis Ridge. This may involve a short step of ice or fifth-class rock.

The upper headwall variation climbs the long, steep snowface left of the large buttressed rock. This route crosses a crevasse or bergschrund before climbing the 50-degree face. Small rock bands near the top are easy to climb in reaching upper Curtis Ridge.

From 13,800 feet on the top of Curtis Ridge, cross the broad summit col south to the crater rim and Columbia Crest.

Descent: Descend the Emmons/Winthrop Glaciers route to Camp Schurman.

Emmons/Winthrop Glaciers

The Emmons/Winthrop Glaciers route is Mount Rainier's least technical and second-most popular climb. The climb is longer and more physically demanding than the most popular track, the Ingraham Direct/Disappointment Cleaver. The Emmons/Winthrop route ascends the upper mountain within the broad area where the streams of the two glaciers flow side by side.

Climbers enjoy the approach through old-growth forest and subalpine and alpine terrain. Once on the mountain, the climb requires good glacier navigation skills as teams weave in and around immense crevasses. Opaque blue glacial ice, towering seracs, cavernous crevasses, and suspect snow bridges dot the route. The Emmons/Winthrop route makes for excellent, exciting glacier mountaineering.

> **ELEVATION GAIN:** 10,000 feet from White River Campground to Columbia Crest.
>
> **WHAT TO EXPECT:** Glacier travel; 30- to 40-degree snow and ice slopes. Grade II.
>
> **TIME:** 2 to 3 days; 7 to 9 hours from Camp Schurman to the summit, 3 to 4 hours for descent to Camp Schurman.
>
> **SEASON:** Mid-May through September.
>
> **FIRST ASCENT:** Unknown; railroad surveyors may have climbed the route in 1855.
>
> **HIGH CAMP:** Camp Schurman (9,460 feet) or Emmons Flats (9,800 feet).

Since this route is completely on glacier snow, it changes from year to year and season to season, depending on the snowfall, crevasses, and icefalls that

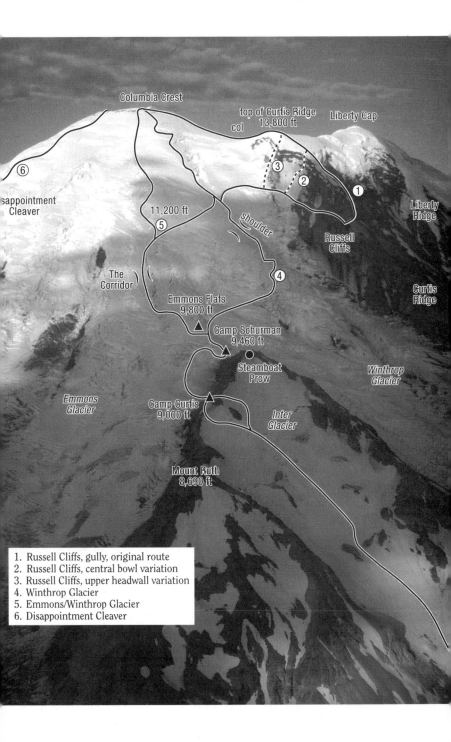

Columbia Crest

top of Curtis Ridge
13,800 ft

col

Liberty Cap

⑥

sappointment
Cleaver

③

②

①

Liberty
Ridge

11,200 ft

⑤

shoulder

Russell
Cliffs

The
Corridor

④

Curtis
Ridge

Emmons Flats
9,800 ft

Camp Schurman
9,460 ft

Steamboat
Prow

Winthrop
Glacier

Emmons
Glacier

Camp Curtis
9,000 ft

Inter
Glacier

Mount Ruth
8,690 ft

1. Russell Cliffs, gully, original route
2. Russell Cliffs, central bowl variation
3. Russell Cliffs, upper headwall variation
4. Winthrop Glacier
5. Emmons/Winthrop Glacier
6. Disappointment Cleaver

determine access to the summit. From Emmons Flats, ascend southerly to the Corridor, a prominent snow slope with fewer crevasses and gentle slopes that rises higher than the rest of the Emmons Glacier. Enter the Corridor between 10,000 and 10,300 feet and ascend to 11,200 feet, where the route becomes steeper (30 to 35 degrees).

From 11,200 feet, the route may take a variety of directions. Ascend gla-

cier slopes through crevasses and seracs, sometimes traversing onto the Winthrop Glacier. The Winthrop frequently has a smooth shoulder above 12,200 feet, with few crevasses and icefalls. This slope can also be icy and is frequently quite hard; carry pickets for use as running protection.

Between 13,500 and 13,700 feet, a bergschrund usually forms at the top of both the Emmons and Winthrop Glaciers. This always creates some fuss, and challenges climbers every year. At any time of the year, it may require downclimbing, steep and icy climbing, exposed traversing, and belays to access the final slopes and the crater rim at 14,250 feet. From the rim, it's a 15-minute walk to Columbia Crest.

Descent: Descend the route.

APPENDIX I
GLOSSARY OF SELECTED MOUNTAINEERING TERMS

Alpine start. An early departure from camp. Climbers get up before dawn and try to complete the ascent before the heat of the day warms snow and ice and increases hazards.

Aspect. The exposure or direction a slope faces. The Emmons Glacier has a northeastern aspect, the Tahoma Glacier a southwestern.

Bergschrund. The uppermost crevasse at the top of a glacier. The bergschrund marks the point at which snow and ice break away from the snowcap and begin moving down the mountain. A bergschrund can pose a serious challenge as climbers try to cross over, through, or around it.

Bollard. A solid mound of snow fashioned by mountaineers to serve as an anchor for the rope.

Buttress. A broad, steep wall, usually below the end of a ridge.

Carry over. To carry all gear to the summit and then descend another route, with no intention of returning to high camp.

Cleaver. A prominent earthy or rocky ridge that divides (cleaves) two glaciers.

Col. A high pass between two summits. On Rainier, the word *col* generally refers to the low points between the mountain's three highest peaks: Columbia Crest, Liberty Cap, and Point Success.

Cornice. Wind-drifted snow piled on a ridge top and often overhanging; a cornice can break off and avalanche.

Couloir. A steep, deep chute usually filled with snow.

Crevasse. A crack or fracture in a glacier, sometimes hundreds of feet deep. Crevasses can be hidden by snow, making them a treacherous hazard. They change shape as the glacier flows down the slope.

Firn, or névé. Old glacial snow.

Fumarole. A vent or hole where hot volcanic gases escape, common along Rainier's summit crater rim.

Gendarme. A rock pinnacle; these features get their name from the French police known for standing straight, like pillars.

Facing page: Silhouetted climber, Steamboat Prow

Glissading. Sliding on one's rear or feet on snow for a rapid descent; it is not recommended on glaciers.

Headwall. The beginning, or "head," of a cirque or basin. Generally a steep wall.

High camp. A high-altitude alpine site where climbers camp before moving on to the summit.

Icefall. A turbulent, broken section of a glacier, composed of crevasses, seracs, and other ever-changing snow features. An icefall typically forms where glaciers move down steep slopes. Icefall also can refer to falling ice, just as rockfall refers to falling rock.

Lenticular cloud. The lens-shaped cloud cap that frequents the summit of Mount Rainier. Formed by condensing moisture as it cools when rising over the summit, these clouds often precede bad weather.

Moat. The gap that is melted between a rock face and an adjoining snowfield or glacier. Moats can be deep, and difficult to cross.

Moraine. The rocky ridge at the base (terminal moraine) and sides (lateral moraine) of a glacier. Moraines, made of an unstable mix of rock and sand deposited by the glacier, mark the glacier's previous terminus.

Nunatak. A terrestrial "island" surrounded by a glacier.

Rime ice. Freezing, wind-blown moisture that collects against objects (rocks, gear, and clothing) and forms opaque ice crystals that extend into the windward side.

Rock band. A continuous rock formation, usually long and narrow. On Rainier, they frequently have snow slopes above and below.

Scree. Loose, rocky debris, usually below cliffs; tough walking.

Serac. A large tower of ice and snow on a glacier. Seracs are usually found around or in icefalls. They make for great ice climbing, but they occasionally fall over, sometimes tumbling for thousands of feet down the glacier.

Short-rope. To tie a climber into the rope close behind a lead climber.

Spindrift. Loose, powdery snow that is easily windblown. Accumulated spindrift can be a substantial avalanche hazard.

Suncups. Melted depressions in the snow, appearing as large, cuplike waves; caused by wind and sun.

Talus. Loose, rocky debris, usually below cliffs; similar to scree, but larger.

Verglas. Rock covered with thin ice.

Wands. Markers used by climbers to indicate a route or cache of gear. These are typically 3-foot-long bamboo garden sticks with highly visible tape on the top.

Whiteout. A condition of limited visibility and flat, deceptive lighting caused by fog, clouds, or storms, preventing safe or accurate navigation and orientation.

APPENDIX II
SUGGESTED READING AND OTHER INFORMATION SOURCES

Barcott, Bruce. *The Measure of a Mountain: Beauty and Terror on Mount Rainier*. Seattle: Sasquatch Books, 1997.

Beckey, Fred. *Cascade Alpine Guide 1: Columbia River to Stevens Pass*. 2nd ed. Seattle: The Mountaineers, 1987.

Graydon, Don, and Kurt Hanson, editors. *Mountaineering: The Freedom of the Hills*. 6th ed. Seattle: The Mountaineers, 1997.

McClung, David, and Peter Schaerer. *The Avalanche Handbook*. Seattle: The Mountaineers, 1997.

Molenaar, Dee. *The Challenge of Rainier*. Seattle: The Mountaineers, 1979.

Selters, Andy. *Glacier Travel and Crevasse Rescue*. 2nd ed. Seattle: The Mountaineers, 1999.

Wilkerson, James. *Medicine for Mountaineering and Other Wilderness Activities*. 4th ed. Seattle: The Mountaineers, 1992.

INFORMATION SOURCES
Mount Rainier National Park
Tahoma Woods
Star Route
Ashford, WA 98304-9751
360-569-2211
e-mail: morainfo@nps.gov
Climbing web site: www.nps.gov/mora/climb.htm

HIGH-CAMP RESERVATIONS
360-569-4453
fax: 360-569-2255
e-mail: mora_wilderness@nps.gov

CAMPGROUND RESERVATIONS
(COUGAR ROCK AND OHANAPECOSH; JULY 1–LABOR DAY)
1-800-365-CAMP

HOTELS IN MOUNT RAINIER NATIONAL PARK (PARADISE INN AND NATIONAL PARK INN)

Mount Rainier Guest Services
P.O. Box 108
Ashford, WA 98304
360-569-2275
www.guestservices.com/rainier

MOUNT RAINIER GUIDE SERVICES

Alpine Ascents International: 206-378-1927   www.alpineascents.com
American Alpine Institute: 206-671-1505   www.mtnguide.com
Cascade Alpine Guides: 425-688-8054   www.cascadealpine.com
Mount Rainier Alpine Guides: 360-825-3773   www.rainierguides.com
Rainier Mountaineering Inc.: 253-627-6242   www.mtrainierguides.com

NORTHWEST WEATHER AND AVALANCHE CENTER

206-526-6677
www.nwac.noaa.gov

INDEX

A

Alpine Ascents International, 23
altitude sickness, 56–59
American Alpine Institute, 23
avalanches, 51–55

B

Beilstein, George, 65, 91
Bertulis, Alex, 148, 163
blue bags (*see* sanitation)
Boulton, Eddie, 164, 166

C

Cadaver Gap, 82, 83
Camp Comfort, 85–87
Camp Hazard, 22, 80, 95-98, 100,
    102–104, 106, 108
Camp Misery, 85, 87
Camp Muir, 22, 62, 64, 79–83
Camp Schurman, 21, 22, 152, 153,
    173, 174, 176–179
campgrounds, 19, 20
Carbon Glacier, 155, 157, 159, 162
Carbon River, 18, 19, 135
Cascade Alpine Guides, 23
Cathedral Gap and Rocks, 82, 83
Central Mowich Face, 78, 125, 132,
    135–144
Central Rib, Willis Wall, 78, 152,
    155, 159–162, 164–167, 169
Columbia Crest, 68–71
Cowlitz Cleaver, 85, 87–90

Cowlitz Glacier, 80, 82, 83
crater rim (*see* Columbia Crest)
Curtis Ridge, 78, 152–155, 162, 169,
    171–173

D

Davis, Dan, 145
descending, 71
Disappointment Cleaver, 78–84, 153
driving instructions (*see* Getting to
    the Park)

E

East Rib, Willis Wall, 78, 152, 155,
    162, 165, 167–170
East Willis Wall, 78, 152, 155, 162,
    169–171
eating, 66, 67
Edmunds Glacier, 138–140
Edmunds Headwall, 78, 125, 132,
    135–141
Emmons Flats, 22, 177–179
Emmons Glacier, 78, 80, 83, 152,
    153, 176–179
equipment and clothing, 28–30

F

Fickle Finger of Success (*see*
    Success Couloirs)
Fuhrer Finger, 78–80, 92, 94–100
Fuhrer Thumb, 78–80, 92, 94–100, 103
Fuller, Fay, 14

G

Getting to the Park, 16-19
Gibraltar Chute, 78–80, 85–89, 92
Gibraltar Ledges, 78–80, 82–88, 92
grading systems, 75, 76
guide services, 22, 23

H

health, 56–61
high altitude illness (*see* altitude sickness)

I

information centers, 15, 16
Ingraham Flats, 22, 82, 83
Ingraham Glacier Direct, 78–84
Inter Glacier, 153, 173, 174, 177, 178

K

Kautz Cleaver, 78–80, 93–95, 100, 106–109, 114, 116
Kautz Glacier, 78-80, 93-95, 97, 100, 102–109
Kautz Headwall, 78–80, 93–95, 97, 100, 103, 105-109
Kautz, Lieutenant August Valentine, 13, 102
Kellogg, Chad, 14

L

Liberty Cap, 69–71
Liberty Ridge, 65, 78, 147, 152–155, 157–160, 162
Liberty Wall Direct, 78, 152, 155–159
Liberty Wall Ice Cap, 78, 150, 152, 155–159
Litch, Dr. Jim (*see also* health), 10
Little Tahoma (11,138 feet), 153

lodging, Mount Rainier Guest Services, 19, 20
Longmire, 16–18, 20, 110
Lower Curtis Ridge, 78, 152, 154, 155

M

Moore, Mark (*see also* weather, avalanches), 10
Mount Rainier Alpine Guides, 23
Mowich Face, 78, 125, 132, 135–146
Mowich Lake, 18, 19, 139
Muir Snowfield, 22, 81
Muir, John, 14

N

National Park Service, The, 15
Nisqually Cleaver, 78–80, 83, 88–92, 100
Nisqually Glacier, 80, 83, 87–92, 94, 100
Nisqually Ice Cliff, 78–80, 83, 88–92, 100
Nisqually Icefall, 78–80, 83, 88, 92, 93, 100
North Mowich Glacier, 136, 137, 144, 147
North Mowich Headwall, 78, 135–139, 143-145, 147
North Mowich Icefall, 78, 135–139, 144–147
Northwest Avalanche Institute, 55
Northwest Weather and Avalanche Center, 45, 55

P

pace, 67, 68
Paradise, 79
passing, 68

permits, 20
Point Success, 69–71
protecting the park, 23, 24
Ptarmigan Ice Cliff, 78, 135, 146–151, 155, 157, 159
Ptarmigan Ridge, 78, 135, 136, 144, 146–151
Puyallup Cleaver, 78, 110, 111, 124–128
Puyallup Glacier, 125, 132

R
Rainier Mountaineering Inc. (RMI), 23, 28, 81
ranger stations, 15, 16
rescues, 42–44
Russell Cliffs, 153, 174–177

S
safety and survival, 37–44, 76
Sanderson, Allen, 172
sanitation, 30, 31
Simonson, Eric, 37, 41, 101
slab avalanches (*see* avalanches)
South Mowich Glacier, 125, 129, 132, 134
South Tahoma Headwall and Glacier, 78, 110–112, 114, 116–119, 121, 127
steam caves, 70, 71
Steamboat Prow, 153, 177, 178
Stevens, General Hazard, 13, 71, 84
Success Cleaver, 78, 106, 108, 110–117
Success Couloirs, 78, 108, 110–117
Success Glacier, 108, 114–116
summit (*see* Columbia Crest)
Sunset Amphitheater Headwall Couloir, 78, 110, 111, 124–132
Sunset Amphitheater Ice Cap, 78, 110, 111, 124–132
Sunset Ridge, 78, 110, 111, 124–127, 129–134, 138

T
Tahoma Cleaver, 63, 78, 110, 111, 116, 118–124, 127
Tahoma Glacier, 78, 110, 111, 121, 124–128
Tahoma Sickle, 78, 111, 121, 124–128
Thermogenesis, 78, 152, 155, 159–163
Thumb Rock, 22, 147, 157, 159, 160, 162

V
Van Trump, Philemon Beecher, 13, 71, 84

W
Wapowety Cleaver, 78, 93–96
Warner, A.C., 14
weather, 45–50
West Rib, Willis Wall, 78, 152, 155, 159–165
Westman, Mark, 137
Westside Road, 16–18, 78, 110, 112, 113, 124
White River, 78, 152–154
Wickwire, Jim, 145, 166, 167
Willis Wall, 78, 152, 155, 160–171
Wilson Glacier Headwall, 78–80, 92, 94, 95, 97–103
Wilson Glacier, 80, 97–100, 103
winter climbing, 32, 34, 35
Winthrop Glacier, 78, 152, 153, 173–179

ABOUT THE AUTHOR

Mike Gauthier started backpacking in the Washington wilderness at age eleven. He began his career in the National Park Service as a volunteer backcountry ranger in Olympic National Park. Ten years ago, he joined the climbing staff at Mount Rainier, where he is now the Lead Climbing Ranger. Mike has summited Mount Rainier over 150 times by twenty-four different routes in all seasons and under all conditions. He regularly conducts workshops in mountain and rope rescue techniques, cold weather survival skills, backcountry snowboarding, and avalanche awareness. In 1998 he was designated a Wilderness Rescue Hero by the American Red Cross.

In addition to his activities at Mount Rainier, he has led three expeditions to Alaska's Mount McKinley, and he is an avid snowboarder, rock climber, and photographer. His photographic artwork is on permanent display in the National Park Inn, Longmire, Washington, and on the web at www.crevasse.com. Mike lives in Mount Rainier National Park.

THE MOUNTAINEERS, founded in 1906, is a nonprofit outdoor activity and conservation club, whose mission is "to explore, study, preserve, and enjoy the natural beauty of the outdoors. . . . " Based in Seattle, Washington, the club is now the third-largest such organization in the United States, with 15,000 members and five branches throughout Washington State.

The Mountaineers sponsors both classes and year-round outdoor activities in the Pacific Northwest, which include hiking, mountain climbing, ski-touring, snowshoeing, bicycling, camping, kayaking and canoeing, nature study, sailing, and adventure travel. The club's conservation division supports environmental causes through educational activities, sponsoring legislation, and presenting informational programs. All club activities are led by skilled, experienced volunteers, who are dedicated to promoting safe and responsible enjoyment and preservation of the outdoors.

If you would like to participate in these organized outdoor activities or the club's programs, consider a membership in The Mountaineers. For information and an application, write or call The Mountaineers, Club Headquarters, 300 Third Avenue West, Seattle, Washington 98119; (206) 284-6310.

The Mountaineers Books, an active, nonprofit publishing program of the club, produces guidebooks, instructional texts, historical works, natural history guides, and works on environmental conservation. All books produced by The Mountaineers are aimed at fulfilling the club's mission.

Send or call for our catalog of more than 300 outdoor titles:

 The Mountaineers Books
1001 SW Klickitat Way, Suite 201
Seattle, WA 98134
800-553-4453
mbooks@mountaineers.org
www.mountaineersbooks.org

Other titles you may enjoy from The Mountaineers:

MOUNTAINEERING: The Freedom of the Hills, 6th Edition, *The Mountaineers*
The completely revised and expanded edition of the best-selling mountaineering book of all time—required reading for all climbers.

SELECTED CLIMBS IN THE CASCADES, *Jim Nelson and Peter Potterfield*
Detailed, illustrated guide to 78 climbing routes in Washington's Cascades. Opportunities for climbers of all skill levels, whether you're looking for the easiest way up Mount Adams or yearning for the wildest rock routes in the North Cascades.

GOING HIGHER: Oxygen, Man, and Mountains, *Charles Houston, M.D.*
The classic study of survival at high altitudes. Completely revised to cover the most important findings of the last ten years—including why understanding hypoxia is so important for the management of the many illnesses and injuries that affect millions of people at sea level.

AVALANCHE SAFETY FOR SKIERS AND CLIMBERS, 2nd Edition, *Tony Daffern*
A thoroughly illustrated manual on avoidance of avalanche hazard by good routefinding and recognition of dangerous slopes. Essential reading for climbers, backcountry powderhounds, ski tourers, or anyone who ventures into avalanche terrain.

EXTREME ALPINISM: Climbing Light, Fast, and High, *Mark F. Twight and James Martin*
A full-color master class on extreme alpine climbing by one of the world's elite mountaineers. Delivers an expert dose of reality and practical techniques for advanced climbers.

THE BEST OF ROCK & ICE: An Anthology, *Edited by Dougald MacDonald*
Rock & Ice magazine's finest stories collected in one volume. Includes stories by Greg Child, Jim Bridwell, Alison Osius, and Andrew Todhunter.

GLACIER TRAVEL AND CREVASSE RESCUE, 2nd Edition, *Andy Selters*
A comprehensive course in understanding glaciers, crossing them, avoiding crevasses, and rescuing crevasse victims. Includes expanded and updated information on technical improvements and safety.